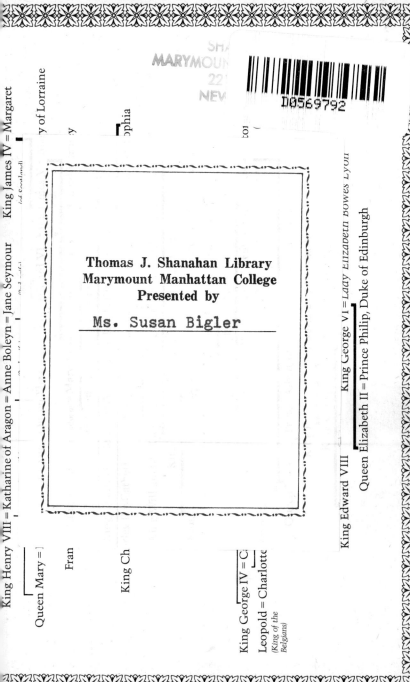

King Henry VIII = Katharine of Aragon = Anne Boleyn = Jane Seymour   King James IV = Margaret

y of Lorraine

phia

King George VI = Lady Elizabeth Bowes Lyon

Queen Elizabeth II = Prince Philip, Duke of Edinburgh

King Edward VIII

Queen Mary =]

Fran

King Ch

King George IV = C...

Leopold = Charlotte
(King of the
Belgians)

THE BRITISH MONARCHY
IN COLOUR

Windsor Castle

THE BRITISH
MONARCHY
IN COLOUR

JOHN BROOKE-LITTLE
Richmond Herald of Arms
MVO, MA, FSA

BLANDFORD PRESS
POOLE   DORSET

Blandford Press Ltd.
Link House, West Street,
Poole, Dorset BH15 1LL

First published 1976

Set in 10pt Bembo 1½pt leaded

Colour section printed by Colour Reproductions, Billericay
Text printed and bound by Butler and Tanner Ltd., Frome, Somerset

ISBN 0 7137 0774 7 (cased)

CONTENTS

Dedication
For Philip, Clare, Leo and Merlin

ACKNOWLEDGEMENTS

The author and publisher gratefully acknowledge all those who have helped in the preparation of this book. These include Ronald Allison, Press Secretary to The Queen, and Mrs Michael Wall, Assistant Press Secretary, for their assistance and co-operation; also Chris Ellis, G. N. Georgano, Kenneth Munson and O. S. Nock for their specialist contributions on Royal Yachts, Royal Cars, Royal Aircraft and Royal Trains respectively.

For the colour section, acknowledgement is due as follows:

To Photographie Giraudon, Paris, for the reproductions from the Bayeux Tapestry (**1** and **2**); to the National Gallery, London, for the Triptych (**3**); to the National Portrait Gallery, London, for the royal portraits (**4–22**); to the Lord Brownlow for the portrait of King Edward VIII (**23**); to the Angus District Council and the estate of the late Frank Beresford for the portrait of King George VI (**24**); to Pietro Annigoni and the Most Worshipful Company of Fishmongers for the portrait of H.M. The Queen (**25**); to David Hopkinson (**26–30, 33**), Chris Collins (**31**) and Araminta Ross (**34**) for paintings of coats of arms; to the College of Arms for the grant of Arms (**36**); Keystone Press Agency Ltd. (**39, 41, 46, 50, 51, 52, 53, 54, 57, 58, 61, 62, 63, 64, 69, 73, 74, 75, 77, 80, 81, 82**); to Paul Popper Ltd. (Popperfoto) (**38, 49, 55, 56, 59, 60, 67, 68, 70, 71, 76, 78**); to the Press Association Ltd. (**40**); to John Freeman for photographs of portraits of Members of the Household (**41–44**); to the Controller of Her Majesty's Stationery Office for the Crown copyright photograph of the Coronation regalia (**45**); to John Wood for paintings of the Coronation coach and door panel (**47** and **48**); to

Camera Press Ltd. (**65, 66, 79**); to Clifford and Wendy Meadway for the painting of the locomotive (**72**).

Acknowledgement is also due as follows for the illustrations in the text pages:

To Her Majesty the Queen for Her gracious permission to include the drawing of the Coronation Chair (p. 34) and the illustrations of the royal residences as used by Queen Victoria on Her personal writing paper (i and Chapter 7); to the British Museum, London, for the Coins of Saxon Kings (p. 17); to Sir Anthony Wagner, R. O. Dennys and the author for the Royal Arms (p. 20) and Arms of the Prince of Wales (p. 31); to the Keystone Press Agency Ltd., for effigy (p. 134); to the Press Association Ltd., Coronation photograph (pp. 48–49); to the National Motor Museum for the drawing of the first royal motor drive (p. 189); to Hawker Siddeley for photograph (p. 196).

AUTHOR'S PREFACE

When I was invited to write this book I had natural reservations as to my ability to tackle such an overwhelming subject in a relatively small book. What I did not have were any reservations as to whether the market could stand yet another book on monarchy, for my experience has been that there is unlimited interest in the subject. I did however realise that for my book to have any value it would have to be a little different from others in the same field.

As I am neither jingoistic about monarchy nor sentimental about the royal family, I have not attempted a triumphalistic book. Rather I have tried, by a series of what may seem somewhat disconnected essays, to demonstrate that the monarchy is an especial, enduring and inestimably important part of the constitution: that it is what it is because it has proved itself to be versatile and adaptable, and finally, that the royal family has, in fact, adapted itself admirably to the mutable and mobile political and social scene.

In the past, monarchs have sometimes been intransigent, or at least insensitive to the winds of change, but in the last analysis they have been unable to resist the will of the people. Graciously or ungraciously they have ultimately honoured the contract between monarch and people, which is the heart and core of the monarchical system.

Even as I write, the press is wallowing in editorials, articles and individual opinions on the breakdown of the marriage of Princess Margaret and Lord Snowdon, a few even going so far as to suggest that this domestic tragedy has shaken the foundations of the monarchy. They forget that similar difficulties have occurred throughout history. The monarchy has survived all the seven deadly sins and a few more; it is therefore hardly likely, however distressing this may be to the Queen herself and many of her loyal subjects, that the monarchy will so much as quiver. This is why, in this book, I have mingled the bad with the good and the past with the present in a shameless *pot pourri*, hoping that by doing so I have helped to put monarch and monarchy into some sort of historical perspective.

Loyalty, when it is critical, sympathetic and responsible, is a most admirably quality, but when it is uninformed, sentimental and irrational, it is so mercurial as to be a weakness. I hope my loyalty is not the insubstantial sort; certain it is that in my view monarchy in Great Britain and within the Commonwealth is synonymous with peaceful coexistence and ordered living, so long may it continue and long may the Queen live to add her magic lustre to the greatest Crown in the world.

Heyford House, 1976

John Brooke Little
Richmond

1

BRITISH MONARCHY

Kings and emperors are generally regarded as a race apart, to be judged by their usefulness or their performance. In a sense this is a fair judgement as they are set apart by society for a purpose, a purpose which has varied from country to country and age to age.

Yet kingship is really only an extension of the natural law by which a man and woman come together to procreate children, the resultant community of persons being called a family. It is the family which, although attacked by some modern sociologists, has formed the basic unit of society from time immemorial.

In the family each member has his place. The father is the protector and producer whilst the mother keeps the home. The children, according to their sex, assist their parents until they flee the nest and set up families of their own. However much people may try to isolate individuals in society and apportion the jobs of males and females indifferently among them, blood and nature remain. Children inherit genes from their parents and rely on the family for some sort of innate companionship, help and protection. Men and women are physically and emotionally different and the majority of them will gravitate towards those activities for which they are naturally best equipped and at which perforce they excel.

Families in primitive society grouped together to form larger communities in order the better to protect themselves and, by a division of labour, to lead more satisfying lives. Just as the father is head of the family, so communities of families acknowledged a father or leader. This leader, because of his obligations to his community, received from it

[1]

a measure of deference and tribute which, albeit to a very small extent, set him apart. This deference naturally extended to his immediate kin, from whom the community might therefore reasonably be expected to choose the next leader. In this way an élite or ruling class evolved and the seeds of kingship were sown.

Small communities were overcome by larger ones, seeking better economic conditions; thus groups and tribes of nomadic men emerged. These eventually found fertile lands where they could settle and build villages and their leaders became more than providers, protectors and captains, they were also law-givers, judges and even priests. The leader of a tribe exercised over his tribe the same sort of dominion as did the head of the family. He was the father of his tribe. The paternal nature of the leader is symbolised by the shepherd's crook and the corn flail, which were the regalia of the ancient Egyptian kings, indicating that they led and fed their people.

So families made up communities, which united into tribes, which settled and formed nations. Sometimes these split and divided but they often found it prudent to acknowledge one of their number as head king. A modern example of such dynastic division, all under the suzerainty of an emperor, was the Holy Roman Empire. The Electors of the Empire, of which for a while King George III was one, elected the Emperor. In fact, the election invariably fell on the heir of the imperial Austrian family, illustrating how kingship, although often technically elective, for convenience and the avoidance of wars and schisms, usually follows predictable hereditary patterns.

Because, for hundreds of years, most European monarchies have descended in tail male or tail general, that is to heirs male in order of primogeniture as in France, or to heirs female failing heirs male as in England and Scotland, it is not realised that there have been many other types of succession. What most of these have in common is that the successor should have the blood of the founder of the dynasty.

In some communities the keeper of the home was considered more important than the provider and there are African tribes where queens were succeeded only by females. As far as the inheritance of genes is concerned there is some logic here for it is usually known who mothered a child, but only the mother knows who fathered it.

[2]

A child king was always a danger as his power could easily be usurped and civil war ensue. For this reason, the ancient Gaels sometimes chose an older member of the royal dynasty to succeed in preference to a child. In elective monarchies, such as the Holy Roman Empire, mentioned above, the person elected was, if not heir male or heir general, at least a member of the royal dynasty.

In cases where a throne has been won by conquest and the people have elected or accepted the conqueror as founder of a new dynasty, the new king frequently sought to ally himself as swiftly as possible with the ancient dynasty he had upset. King Henry VII let no grass grow under his feet after parliament had enacted that the crown rightfully belonged to him and the heirs of his body, for within a year of ascending the throne, he had married Elizabeth, eldest daughter and co-heir of King Edward IV, the Yorkist king. It is usually stated that this marriage united the houses of York and Lancaster; this is true politically but not dynastically, for Henry VII was not the head of the House of Lancaster, but the son of a great-grand-daughter of John, Duke of Beaufort, illegitimate son of John of Gaunt, who had been legitimated for all purposes save succession to the throne.

Henry's marriage ensured that his descendants, upon whom the succession had been secured, would have the blood of the senior legitimate line of Plantagenet.

It is this preoccupation with the inheritance of the royal blood that has led many dynastics to marry within the ranks of royalty. The ancient Egyptian Ptolemys were even more eclectic and not only married within their own dynasty, but within their immediate family circle. Ptolemy VI married his sister Cleopatra II and their brother Ptolemy VII married their daughter, Cleopatra III. Their son Ptolemy VIII married his sister Cleopatra V (having previously married another sister) and their son Ptolemy XI married his sister Cleopatra VI. As incestuous a line as ever existed.

In our own royal family, although the sovereign has usually married royal siblings, this has not always been the case. For example, Edward IV married Elizabeth Wydville, four of Henry VIII's wives were the daughters of subjects and James II married Anne Hyde, daughter of the Earl of Clarendon. Such marriages were generally unpopular as a king who married a subject lost, or seemed to lose, something of his impartiality; his stature and that of his dynasty were reduced in the eyes of his people. Today things are different as the monarch, although still set apart from his subjects, is no longer personally identified with the administration of justice, nor does he have the opportunity of granting exceptional favours to his wife's family.

When King George V's sons, the Dukes of York and Gloucester, married commoners there was general rejoicing and the King gladly gave his permission and blessing. He was not to know that Albert, Duke of York, was to become King George VI, but even if he had known, I very much doubt whether it would have made the slightest difference. Knowing King George's opinion of Germans, it is far more likely that he would have objected to an alliance with the daughter of a German princeling than with that of a noble Scottish family.

That King George had to give permission for his son to marry is interesting in itself. The reason for this is to be found in the Royal Marriage Act 1772.

George III was very indignant that his two brothers, Henry Frederick, Duke of Cumberland, and William Henry, Duke of Gloucester, had married commoners. The former married Mrs Anne Horton, a widow, and the latter Maria, bastard daughter of Sir Edward Walpole and widow of Lord Waldegrave. He therefore devised a Bill, which met with much opposition, but which eventually became law, whereby no descendants of George II, other than foreign princesses, could marry without the consent of the sovereign. If over twenty-five years old such royal siblings could marry if no objection were raised by parliament and as long as a year's notice were given to the Privy Council. Marriages contracted contrary to this Act were null and void and the contracting parties were liable to incur the penalties of *praemunire*, namely loss of civil rights, forfeiture of land and goods and imprisonment during the royal pleasure. This Act, which is still in force, was the last Act to impose the excessive penalties of *praemunire*.

This act makes explicit the theory of keeping the royal blood untainted, although it was influenced not so much by a wish to return to ancient principles as by the German precept whereby it was, and in some families still is, considered mandatory that a prince or princess

[4]

marries within the same strata of society. In German and some other royal families marriage to a commoner was permitted, but it was considered morganatic. That meant that the marriage was valid and the issue legitimate, but that such issue was debarred from succession. Earl Mountbatten of Burma's grandfather, Prince Alexander of Hesse and the Rhine, contracted a morganatic marriage with Julia von Hauke, who was later created Princess of Battenburg, but her descendants were debarred from succeeding to the Grand Dukedom of Hesse. In Great Britain there is no such thing as a morganatic marriage. If a member of the royal family marries in defiance of the Royal Marriage Act, the marriage, as has been stated, is null and any children of the marriage are illegitimate.

Queen Victoria's uncle, Augustus, Duke of Sussex, married twice in contravention of the Act, although both his wives were daughters of earls and so not exactly disreputable. His first wife, or more correctly lady, was Lady Augusta Murray. He married her once in Rome and again in London, but the marriage was declared null and void by the Prerogative Court in 1794. His two children by this marriage took the name of d'Este, but neither left descendants. His second lady, Cecilia, was the widow of Sir George Buggin and daughter of the Earl of Arran. Neither the duke nor his ladies were subjected to the penalties of *praemunire*; indeed, it is an interesting reflection on Queen Victoria's character that she created her uncle's mistress, for such she truly was, Duchess of Inverness for life, three years before the old duke died.

The Early British Kings

The characteristics of kingship which I have described are more or less universal. The king is the father figure, set above and apart from his people, who are his family. The British monarchy today is directly descended, not just historically but in actual blood and genes, from the old British tribal chiefs.

The barrows or burial mounds which are a characteristic of parts of southern England are not only curious old graves, they can also be storehouses of history which from time to time yield up great treasures, enriching our knowledge of those shadowy years before history was recorded.

About 1650 B.C. at Normanton Down in north Wiltshire a great chieftain was buried, for when his burial mound was excavated, in it were
found many valuable artefacts. Among these was a ceremonial mace,
clearly the insignia of his office. From this we know that as long before
the birth of Christ as King James I lived after it, tribesmen were honour-
ing their leaders by according them rich burials, thus equipping them
for the life to come.

Until the final Roman conquest of Britain in A.D. 44 most of our
knowledge of the ancient Britons comes from archaeological evidence.
Clearly there were many small kingdoms sometimes grouped together
under head kings, but there is, of course, no written history of the period.
When the Roman emperor Claudius came to Britain in September 43
to administer the *coup de grace* to the British, fleeing before the legions
of Aulus Plautius, we know that he received the submission of eleven
conquered British kings. We also know that seventeen years later it was,
to the amazement of the Roman historian, Tacitus, a woman who led
the great revolt against the corruption and arrogance of the Roman con-
querors. Boudicca, queen of the Icenian tribe from East Anglia, an ama-
zonian lady with a mass of tawny hair falling to her hips, was the heroine
of the day. Tribesmen from all over England followed her lead and
rebelled against their Roman masters. Although in the end the discipline
of the Romans triumphed over the more numerous, but disorganised
British, Boudicca had won a moral victory, as the Romans no longer
treated Britain as another Roman milch cow, but brought peace, law
and order and a measure of civilisation to the country; although it must
always be remembered that the majority of the conquered people were
slaves, not masters. If it is true that the exception proves the rule, Boudicca was the exception, as the British never favoured female rulers and
no other woman ruler makes her mark on the pages of our history until
Queen Mary I ascended the throne in 1553.

For three hundred years Britain enjoyed a period of peace as a limb
of one of the greatest empires the world has ever known, an empire
where the emperor himself was often deified, becoming a god, even
in his lifetime.

But the empire crumbled; it was too vast, incursions from without
and corruption and dissentions from within destroyed it. Britain was

attacked from the east by Saxons, from the west by Scots from Ireland, from the north by Picts. The great wall, built at the command of the Emperor Hadrian at the beginning of the second century to keep the barbarians out of Roman Britain, let through the Picts, simply because the Romans could no longer man the garrisons. Everywhere the invaders took advantage of the ever-diminishing Roman forces, until in 410 a new Saxon invasion encouraged many of the Britons to revolt; the Roman towns were left to their fate by the Emperor Honorius and the Roman occupation of Britain was over.

For the history of the succeeding centuries we have to rely on the accounts of the historians Gildas and Bede, legend and the ever-increasing treasures exposed by the archaeologists. Broadly speaking, the invading Anglo-Saxons, Frisians and Jutes were from those parts of Germany and Schleswig outside the Roman empire. They were pagans and brought with them a totally different way of life to that established by the Romans, one of whose religions was Christianity.

The native British, although now bereft of Roman protection, put up a stout fight against the invaders. This was the age of King Arthur, a leader of the British resistance, whom legend and fable have made into a great king, woven about with the mystery of magic and mysticism. But whoever Arthur was, and whether or not he held court at Cadbury Castle in Somerset, now thought by some to be the Camelot of the Arthurian legends, it is certainly true that the British kept the pagans at bay for a hundred and fifty years. It was not until about the year 600 that the Saxons finally pushed the British back into Wales and Cornwall and established a number of small kingdoms in the rest of Britain.

In the north the Scots, who came from Ireland not Scotland, settled in the territory between the Clyde and the Forth, the land north of which was inhabited by the Picts. The leader of the Scots was Fergus the Great, who died in 501. He was the ancestor of King Eochaid the Venomous, who married a Pictish princess. Their son King Alpin and his son Kenneth mac Alpin united the Picts and the Scots as one nation. From Alpin are descended the kings of Scots, who gave their name to the northern part of Britain.

The old Celtic Britons, carrying with them the flame of Christianity, a legacy of Roman times, settled in Wales and Cornwall. The nursery rhyme tells us that Old King Cole was a merry old soul, which may or may not have been true. Certainly his Celtic name Coel hen godibog, Coel the old adulterer, suggests that he led a less than dull life, but he is essentially a legendary figure, said to have sired a daughter Vala, who married the British king Cunedda, whose descendants ruled in the north Welsh principality of Gwynedd. In the ninth century Ethil, heiress of the princes of Gwynedd, married Prince Gwriad of the Isle of Man, and their grandson Rhodi Mawr, who was killed in 878, was the first prince to unite most of Wales. Although this unity was short-lived it was a prince of his line, Llywelyn the Great, who became ruler of all Wales and whose grandson, Llywelyn ap Gruffydd, was recognised as Prince of Wales by King Henry III in 1267.

The Anglo-Saxon kings were almost all descended, by a tradition which cannot be established or otherwise, from the great pagan storm-god Woden. They ruled in Bernicia, Deira, Lindsey, Mercia, East Anglia and Wessex, the greatest kingdoms being those of Wessex and Mercia.

Although various factors militated towards the formation of a united kingdom, the most significant was the conversion of the pagan Saxons to Christianity by St Augustine at the beginning of the seventh century. This meant that the Celts in Wales and the Saxons in England all subscribed to one faith and one moral code. It is true that there were differences between the Celtic Church and the newly established English Church, but these were soon resolved.

The fact that England had become a Christian country, albeit still made up of a number of small kingdoms, is important in that when, in 793, Vikings from Norway landed on Holy Island, looted the ancient monastery of Lindisfarne, the resting place of St Cuthbert, and enslaved the monks, it horrified the whole people of England.

Just over fifty years later, the Danes invaded and once again the English, under Aethelred and his brother Alfred, united to subdue and confine them. So a nation was forged by threats from beyond the seas and the necessity of defending not just life, limb and property, but also a single faith.

Coronation

The essentially Christian character of the monarchy is made manifest in the ceremony of coronation. From time immemorial appointment to high office or estate has been accompanied by some form of ritual induction. Naturally, inauguration to the highest estate, that of king, argues an elaborate ceremony, especially as the mystery and divinity of kingship needs to be symbolised, just as much as the duties of a monarch. Principal elements in the ritual of king-making have been the oath, the enthroning, the investing with symbolic clothes and regalia, sacrifice and anointing. We know that there were Christian ceremonies of inauguration or coronation in the Saxon kingdoms, but no account of these has survived. Egfrith, son of Offa, King of Mercia, was anointed and crowned as successor to his father in 785, but what form the ceremony took is not known.

The first English coronation *ordo* was that compiled by St Dunstan for the coronation of King Eadgar at Bath in 973. Eadgar was the great-grandson of Alfred and grandfather of Edward the Confessor. This service contained the principal elements of the present coronation ritual. The king took an oath, received homage, was anointed, invested with a ring, sword, crown, sceptre and rod and was enthroned. The whole ceremony was incorporated within the sacrifice of the Mass. Thus pre-Christian rituals were incorporated in an essentially Christian service. Eadgar swore to guard the Church of God, forbid violence and wrong and to keep justice, judgement and mercy, but of all the elements of the ceremony, that of anointing was the most significant. Originally a pre-Christian ceremony by which oil, like embalming oil, gave the anointed an eternal character, it symbolised rebirth, as it now does in the Christian Church, so that the holy oil revivifies the king and sets him apart from other men, as one hallowed by God to rule. Aelfric, writing in the early eleventh century, states: 'No man can make himself a king, but the people have the choice to select as king whom they please; but after he is consecrated king, then he has dominion over the people and they cannot shake his yoke from off their necks.'

This view of kingship was later enshrined in the doctrine of the divine right of kings, which led ultimately to the execution of Charles I and the only suspension of monarchical government our country has ever known.

The sacramental nature of kingship satisfied both king and people. It gave the king a divine authority which could stand him in good stead and it gave the people a sense of stability, which, although it was for better or for worse, was inevitably better than sailing in a ship without a helmsman, no matter how bad a navigator that helmsman might be.

The Monarchy after the Conquest

William the Conqueror was a realist. He established a tenuous legal title to the throne, but essentially he acquired it by sheer force of arms. Once established he was anointed king and so had the undoubted right to rule. When he did, his second son became king as William II and on his death the Conqueror's youngest son Henry was crowned, but not before the eldest son, Robert, Duke of Normandy, had challenged his right to the throne. On Henry's death a situation arose which eloquently illustrated the elective nature of the monarchy. There was nothing sacred about the laws of succession if expediency dictated a devious path. Henry had an almost legendary number of illegitimate children, but his only legitimate daughter was Matilda, widow of the Emperor Henry V of Germany and wife of the unpopular Geoffrey, Count of Anjou. But the English did not want a woman on the throne, so even although Matilda was the only designated heir of the king, the election lighted on Matilda's popular cousin Stephen, third son of King Henry's sister Adela, Countess of Blois. It is not for nothing that a chronicler dubs Stephen's reign as that of 'nineteen long winters when God and his saints slept', so that when he died, once again the succession deviated and, passing over Stephen's only surviving son and daughter, lighted on Matilda's son Henry, whom Stephen had accepted as his adopted son and heir at the Treaty of Winchester in 1153.

When Henry II came to the throne in 1154, he was already Duke of Normandy, Count of Anjou and, in the right of Eleanor his wife, Lord of Acquitaine. This meant that more and more of the business of government, especially that of the treasury and judiciary, had to be delegated. However, it would be a mistake to see this delegation as an erosion of royal power. The king's prerogative remained intact, although obviously in delegation there lurked a menace for the future of absolute monarchy.

The first hint of this menace came when King John was forced to agree to Magna Carta. That the Great Council could so force the king's hand, although he doubtless considered it no more than a staying action, was one significant thing; that Magna Carta promulgated the doctrine that the king ruled under the law was another and perhaps more far-reaching consequence of the events which took place at Runnymede on 15 June 1215. A new element was introduced into the conception of monarchy, that of contract. If the king ruled according to law, it was treason for a subject to rebel, but if he acted above or outside the law, his subjects were released from their allegience and could morally over-throw the king.

Over the ensuing centuries, the part played in government by the king's subjects grew steadily. It was a wise king, such as Edward I, who realised that by according a measure of involvement in government to all his people, he could preserve a balance of power and, at the same time, gain grass-roots support for the system of monarchy and the person of the monarch. Simon de Montfort's convention of knights from the shires and burgesses from the towns may not have instituted a House of Commons, as is sometimes asserted, but it created a precedent and gave future kings an idea as to how the people could be wooed and wooed to some advantage, especially financially.

The first king to suffer from the effects of Magna Carta was the unfor-tunate Edward II. His behaviour invited and obtained in no mean measure the censure of the nobles who, deciding that the king had broken his contract to rule, considered themselves absolved from the allegiance they had vowed to him. He was deposed and murdered. It may be that the breaking of the royal contract should rightly end in the deposition of the sovereign, but his murder is another thing alto-gether. Weak and feeble as Edward surely was, he was also the anointed king and his murder sent a shiver of horror through the nation and led his son Edward to avenge his unwise father's horrific death.

Is Edward's sad reign a weighty criticism of the system of inheritance strictly by order of male primogeniture? A system which, as has been seen, was not fully accepted in Norman times. I suggest that although the system has its obvious disadvantages, it is far better than introducing an element of choice, even from among the senior members of the blood royal. Walter Bagehot wrote pessimistically of the sort of monarchs an hereditary system might produce—'a constitutional sovereign must in the common course of government be a man of but common ability'— yet an elective monarchy has less charms for him—'politics would offer a prize too dazzling for mankind; clever base people would strive for it and stupid base people would envy it'.

Richard II suffered the same fate as Edward II, being murdered in Pontefract Castle, his throne having been seized by Henry Bolingbroke, who was not heir to the throne according to the laws of primogeniture, if it is accepted that the succession could be transmitted through a female. Richard had no children. His father's next brother Lionel of Antwerp was dead, as was his daughter Philippa, Countess of Ulster. However, Philippa had a son Roger, Earl of March, whom Richard II had declared his heir.

Henry won the throne by conquest, but claimed it essentially by right of blood, although constitutional historians also insist that election by the people was an integral part of his claim. This is what Henry said about it: '*In the name of God, I Henry of Lancaster, challenge this realm, this crown, and all the members and appurtenances thereof, as by the right blood coming of King Henry* [i.e. Henry III], *and through that right that God of his grace hath sent me, with the help of my kin and my friends, to recover it, the which realm was in point to be undone for default of governance and undoing of the laws.*'

In fact, of course, 'possession is nine points of the law', especially when the possessor has been anointed king and made, by oath, his contract with his people.

History repeated itself when, in 1485, Henry Tudor, Earl of Richmond, led a rebellion against Richard III, the last Yorkist king, and by defeating him at the Battle of Bosworth ended a sad era of English history brought about more by misfortune than because there was anything wrong with the actual system of the monarchy. For the fifteenth century seemed an age of promise. Henry IV and Henry V were strong kings: they relied more and more on their Council and on Parliament and might have led England peacefully forward into the Renaissance, but it was not to be. The early death of Henry V argued a long minority for his weak and pious son Henry VI. The result was the inevitable jockeying for power, ending in the Wars of the Roses.

Henry Tudor, crowned as Henry VII of England, was essentially king for the same reason as his namesake, Henry IV, that is because he was a strong man and so took possession of the throne. But he was not a tyrant; his strength, ability, financial acumen and personal rule were just what his subjects wanted.

Even if a most despicable person is able to give peace and prosperity without inflicting too many wounds he will be welcomed with open arms, particularly if he comes to the rescue of a bankrupt, war-torn country.

So Henry was welcomed and, although an absolute ruler in fact, in theory he continued to develop what gave the appearance of being a ministerial and parliamentary form of government. There was shadow without substance, but the shadow found favour.

Henry VIII was more like his father than is often appreciated. He had the same intelligence and realised that he could do more and that more safely if he acted within constitutional bounds. His divorces, his seizure of church lands and 'take over' of the Church in England were done through parliament. The king may have been the master of parliament rather than *vice versa*, but the formality of consultation was observed. It only needed a weak monarch for the roles of king and parliament to be reversed, so used were the latter to having the sense and feel of exercising power. This, of course, is what happened. The country survived the short minority of Edward VI and the disastrous but mercifully also brief rule of Mary I, to the triumphant rule of Elizabeth I, triumphant for England, the crown and the cult of monarchy. Elizabeth ruled as surely as her father, but, even more than he, she was identified with England and with the interests of her subjects.

I suppose, as others have supposed before me, that the Civil War was inevitable because of the characters of James I and his son Charles I. When the Stuarts came to the throne on Elizabeth's death in 1603 they were foreigners from a foreign land. Even today Scotland tilts a lance for independence, but in 1603 it was a separate kingdom and its king, James VI, was used to different laws and customs. He could not be expected to understand the evolution of parliament under the powerful yet subtle rule of the Tudors. He underrated the English and that proved fatal. This is not the place to detail the events which led inexorably towards civil conflict. Sufficient to state that on the one hand parliament sought more and more to have a real voice in the running of the country, whilst on the other James I openly declared his belief in the divine right of kings. People had always accepted the fact that the anointed monarch was a person set apart by God to rule justly and wisely under the law, but they were not prepared to swallow James's argument, which cannot be more unequivocally nor more eloquently related than in his own words. In a speech to his first parliament, he declared his hand thus:

'The state of monarchy is the supremest thing upon earth: for kings are not only God's lieutenants upon earth and sit upon God's throne, but even by God himself they are called gods. As to dispute what God may do is blasphemy, so it is sedition in subjects to dispute what a king may do in the height of his power.'

Had James's son Charles held more liberal views than his father, the situation might have been saved, but he did not. Because he ended upon the scaffold he has been hailed by some as a martyr, but the golden rays of his martyr's crown should not blind us to the sad truth that he was a silly, obstinate man. He tried to subvert justice, and rule without parliament. The result was that on 27 January 1648/9 Charles was sentenced to be 'put to death by the severing of his head from his body'.

Absolute monarchy was over. Charles II restored to the throne, though not a modern constitutional monarch, was much more like our modern conception of a popular monarch. He was a hero king, representing in his person the ideals, not at that time always very elevating ones, of his people.

Constitutional Monarchy

It seems odd to us today that the king who sought to free his Catholic subjects from the penalties the law imposed on them, should they not conform to the established church in which they did not believe, should lose his throne. But this is what happened; James II acted as he wanted, without consulting parliament. The days were past when this could be done with impunity. James fled the country with his young son. Certain notable men invited William of Orange, the husband of James's daughter Mary, to accept the throne. William and Mary became joint sovereigns and, to make the constitutional position quite clear for the future, parliament passed three important Acts. These Acts legislated that the sovereign must be a member of the Church of England, must swear an oath at his coronation to govern 'according to the statutes in Parliament agreed on' and to 'maintain the laws of God, the true profession of the Gospel, and the Protestant reformed religion established by law'. The other act was the Act of Settlement. This further established the Protestant religion and provided for the succession to the throne by declaring Princess Sophia, Electress and Duchess Dowager of Hanover, next in succession to the throne after William and Mary's issue and Mary's sister Anne of Denmark and her issue.

As it turned out, neither Mary nor Anne had any surviving children, so the succession passed to George, son of Princess Sophia, who had died less than two months before Queen Anne in June 1714. This was sad, as Sophia was an intelligent, tolerant woman, who loved England and would have mounted the throne more delicately and gracefully and consequently more acceptably than her insensitive son.

With the advent of the Hanoverians the monarchy underwent a subtle yet noticeable change. The mystique of kingship began to fade. The hereditary succession had been broken by the will of the people and what appeared to be a totally foreign dynasty had arrived to reign over, yet less and less to rule, the British.

Until 1714 the kings of England had 'touched' for the King's Evil, which was a tubercular condition of the neck, also called scrofula. It is said that King Charles II touched over 100,000 sufferers, but George I discontinued 'touching'. In a way, this abandonment of an ancient practice is symbolic of the change in the attitude of the monarch, a definite move from the romantic towards the practical.

Politically the Hanoverian period saw the forceful emergence of parliament as the ruling body, the king becoming more and more what we call a constitutional monarch—that is, one with notional powers, but no real authority. When George IV came to the throne in 1820 it would have been quite possible for the process of government to have continued without the support and approval of the monarch. Yet it would be wrong to jump to the conclusion that the monarch, because he had become technically unnecessary, was therefore useless. Because the crown remained and is still an integral part of the constitution, the person who wears it cannot help but influence the running of the country. We are fortunate that from the accession of Queen Victoria this influence has been benign and advantageous. The doctrine that the sovereign has the right to be consulted and the duty to encourage and advise is accepted, not only as being constitutionally unexceptionable, but also useful and sensible.

This does not mean that the monarch has not invited criticism. Queen Victoria's complete retirement from her public duties, and her refusal to delegate any aspects of sovereignty to her son after Prince Albert's death, created what Gladstone called 'a great crisis of royalty'. Joseph Chamberlain called for a republic and it required all Gladstone's ability and later the charm of Benjamin Disraeli to persuade the Queen to abandon, to some extent at least, her life of seclusion. This she did and ended her long reign in a blaze of glory, whilst the wealth and prestige of the country were at their zenith. These were indeed the imperial years and the Queen was the symbol and embodiment of the far-flung empire, upon whom the affections of her people were unquestionably centred.

Yet, just as the monarchy basks in the adulation of the populace when it is fulfilling the unwritten and unspoken role required of it at any given moment, the same people will turn against it at the first sign of discord. The abdication crisis of 1936, had it been prolonged, could well have heralded the end of the monarchy. The masses have ever shown themselves volatile, unversed in history, pragmatic and ungrateful. Yet there is at the heart of the country a hard core of wise and careful people, who realise that all human institutions are imperfect. They know that monarchy must have its set-backs like every other institution but that the idea of monarchy is too valuable an asset to throw overboard at the first sign of trouble; it is a poor surgeon who amputates a leg to cure a chilblain.

The Value of Monarchy

Why is monarchy such a valuable institution? This is a valid and important question, for most of the leading countries of the world survive

Echbeorht, King of Wessex, A.D. 802–838(?)
Canterbury mint

Alfred, King of Wessex, A.D. 871–901 (Alfred the Great)
London mint

Aethelred II, King of England, A.D. 979–1016
Thetford mint

Edward the Confessor, King of England, A.D. 1042–1066
Wallingford mint

Silver pennies of four Saxon kings

[17]

without kings and queens. I am sure it is fair to say that monarchy is not necessarily the right institution for every country, although many countries who have abandoned their monarchs are now envious of our royal family. I believe, however, that it is right for the Commonwealth. Our monarchy, as I hope I have shown, is part of a continuing tradition, which has survived many a crisis and from generation to generation has adapted itself to the needs of the country.

In the first place, the monarch is a living symbol; a symbol of continuity, of the ideas, ideals and aspirations of his subjects, of national unity, of the commonwealth family and of order, no matter how fiercely the political battles rage. In the second place, it provides an object, and a living object, on which the loyalty of all can be focused and centred without fear of criticism on political, religious or ethnic grounds; the monarch is consecrated to the service of the nation; the monarch *is* the nation. In the third place the monarchy is glamorous; the traditional ceremonies which the sovereign performs gives a touch of grandeur, elegance and colour to life, which leaves only the philistine unmoved. Our royal occasions are the envy of other nations, for in themselves they symbolise that quality of permanence for which most people crave at some point in their lives.

Lastly, blessed with a royal family which really cares about people and the fate of the nation and which, for as long as most of us can remember, has sacrificed personal pleasure to public duty, we have an asset of incalculable value.

Those who try to evaluate the monarchy in terms of hard cash look only at the expenditure. They should study the other side of the balance sheet and their narrow, shopkeeper minds would be surprised at what the institution of monarchy earns in terms of actual pounds and pence, not to mention dollars and cents. They would also do well to discover what it costs to keep a president in office, and the cash returns from a president do not begin to compare with those of our monarchy.

There used to be a notice hanging on my tailor's wall which read something like this (I cannot quote verbatim as the firm is now no more): 'There is always a man who will make things a little cheaper than another; those who consider price alone are this man's lawful prey.' We

[18]

might be able to acquire a cut-price president, but this, surely, is not really a consideration which would move the hearts and minds of the intelligent majority of the Queen's loyal, loving and grateful subjects.

The Royal Arms

2

THE ROYAL ARMS

The display of the royal coat of arms is an ancient and enduring way of representing and symbolising the sovereign. In the form of a flag it is flown from buildings when the sovereign is present and worn on ships when he is aboard. It appears behind the judge's bench in every court of law, reminding us that it is the king's justice that is being dispensed. It is often engraved on coins of the realm and at one time was erected in churches to demonstrate loyalty to the Crown. It is used extensively to commemorate events connected with the Crown, from the opening of a new hospital to a stained-glass window in a room where a sovereign once slept, as at Compton Wynyates in Warwickshire. There the arms of Henry VIII, Queen Elizabeth I, King James I and King Charles I remind the visitor that these monarchs rested their limbs in the Royal Bedchamber.

Several grammar schools which were royal foundations use the coat of arms of their founder. Tradesmen who supply goods to the Crown are sometimes permitted to display the royal arms with a suitable sub-scription stating that they are 'By Appointment' to the sovereign.

Royal badges are also found in a wide variety of places, indicating ownership by the Crown or some connexion with it. The Palace of Westminster sports the royal badge of a crowned portcullis, which also appears on the reverse of a penny. The three feathers badge of the heir apparent is on the two-pence piece. The splendid Tudor uniform of the Yeoman of the Guard is embroidered with the crowned Tudor rose badge. If one goes back into history innumerable other royal badges are to be found, being used either to beautify or identify.

Heraldry

Before discussing the various royal arms used by the kings and queens I must briefly relate how coats of arms started.

Norman nobles, who under the feudal system captained their own armies, which they led to the defence of king and country when required, needed to be easily recognised. The custom therefore developed, in the latter part of the twelfth century, of decorating shields, banners and coat armour with simple symbolic devices. Because of their use on coat armour, the padded coat worn over the mail, they were referred to as coats of arms or, more briefly, just arms.

Because it was important that, in the cause of identification, no two people should use the same coat of arms, a measure of control was necessary and this control was exercised by the royal heralds. For this reason the study of coats of arms came to be called heraldry.

The only people who needed to be recognised in battle or in the jousts and tournaments, the mock battles, were the leaders. Thus coats of arms came to be associated with a certain class of people and were regarded by them as emblems of honour and status. As the king is the Fountain of Honour, he naturally has a duty to protect the rights of his noble subjects to their coats of arms and this he does through the Court of Chivalry. This ancient court still exists and can determine causes involving the abuse of coats of arms.

An important characteristic of heraldry is its hereditary nature. Coats of arms descend to all the male descendants of the person who first bore the arms and to the females until they marry. The heralds have the duty of recording who is entitled to what arms and to do this they must obviously know about genealogy, for it is only by proving descent that a right to a coat of arms can be legally established.

Although coats of arms were first used as a means of identification by armed warriors, almost concurrently they were employed in a variety of other ways, the most important being on seals. Today, documents are usually authenticated by being signed, but in the early middle ages few could write and read and there were certainly no handwriting experts who could tell whether or not a signature were a forgery. The accepted way of attesting a deed was by affixing a seal to it. To prevent forgery these seals were elaborately engraved and to aid identification it was usual for a man's seal to be decorated with a representation of his shield of arms, or with an effigy of himself on horseback, bearing his coat of arms. This was an important use of heraldry, but representations of a person's coat of arms were used in many other ways. You have only to visit any ancient cathedral to be overwhelmed by the heraldry displayed on tombs, monuments and in stained glass, commemorating the noble dead. Indeed, it is fair to state that coats of arms were used wherever they could either decorate or identify.

A coat of arms essentially identifies the owner of it. It is a very personal symbol of honour and dignity. There are often occasions when a man wishes to mark his own possessions, but feels that the use of his coat of arms is either impracticable because of its complexity, or unsuitable for one reason or another. For example, a mediaeval leader would not dress up his private army in his own coat of arms as he wore this himself, he would identify them by adorning their jerkins with some simple device known to be his. This device is the badge. Great nobles often had many badges which they used in connexion with their various manors and estates. The king likewise used a variety of badges and different kings tended to favour different badges, often adopting new ones when occasion seemed to demand it. The Tudor rose, a white rose on red, was adopted to symbolise the uniting of the houses of York and Lancaster by the marriage of King Henry VII and Princess Elizabeth of York. King George V commemorated his adoption of the dynastic name of Windsor by assuming a Windsor badge consisting of a representation of the round tower at Windsor Castle enclosed between two branches of oak.

Although heraldry is circumscribed by rules and regulations, these do not necessarily apply to royal heraldry which has, as it were, conventions of its own. The principal difference between royal and personal heraldry is that royal heraldry does not symbolise the family of the king, but his dominions. Thus, when Henry VII came to the throne he did not bear the family arms of Tudor, his paternal family, but bore the same arms as Richard III. So, although the English and British thrones have been sat on by Angevins, Tudors, Stuarts, William of Nassau, Hanoverians and Saxons, monarchs of all these dynasties have borne three golden lions on a red shield for England as part of their royal arms.

The Arms of England

It was Richard I who first used this famous coat, which appears on his second great seal. There is evidence to show that lions in one form or another had been favoured as symbols by some of his ancestors, but none had consistently used a particular coat of arms. In illustration (**26**) Richard's helm, with the fan crest decorated with a lion, is shown because this is how it appears on his seal.

This coat was used by all Richard's successors until Edward III altered the royal arms to symbolise his claim to the French throne. In 1337 he maintained that, on the death of Charles IV without issue in 1328, the throne should have passed to him through his mother Isabella, heiress to Charles and not, as it did, to her first cousin, Philip VI, senior heir in the male line.

The royal style was altered from King of England to *Rex Angliae et Franciae*, King of England and France, and Edward divided the royal shield into four quarters, placing the royal arms of France, a blue field powdered with golden fleurs-de-lys, in the first and last quarters and the arms of England in the other two, giving, according to heraldic lore, pride of place to France. He may have done this to underline his pretensions to the French throne and so annoy the French, but more probably he placed France first because, in the mediaeval hierarchy of kingdoms, France took precedence. In fact, when Philip VI first came to the throne of France, Edward did homage to him for the English possessions in France.

Richard II, although he formally and officially used the same arms as his grandfather, Edward III, on some occasions divided his shield vertically and placed the arms of St Edward the Confessor, to whom he had a particular devotion, on one side and his royal coat of France and England on the other. The Confessor did not, of course, have a coat of arms, as he lived a hundred years before the dawn of heraldry, but the early heralds invented arms for the Saxon and early Norman kings and those for St Edward, a golden cross between five birds on a blue shield, based on the reverse of a penny of his time, were often used to represent him. They are incorporated in the Tudor coat designed for Westminster Abbey, Edward's foundation.

In the illustration, Richard's personal coat is ensigned by a helm on which stands a golden lion on a crimson hat. This device is called the crest and is another hereditary device which became popular in the early fourteenth century. As a crest was actually modelled onto the helmet, when shown pictorially as part of the complete coat of arms, the helm was also shown. For the same reason, the short cloak, called the mantling, which was attached to the helm and possibly helped to deflect sword blows aimed at the back of the neck, was also depicted. The royal mantling was red lined with ermine.

One of Richard's favourite badges was the White Hart, collared with a golden coronet and chained. The artist has used two such harts to support his shield. A hundred years later these supporters came to be regarded as part of the actual coat of arms, but here the painter has simply added them as an artistic whim. Likewise, mottoes were not used beneath coats of arms for some generations to come, so that the inclusion of a supposed favourite aphorism of Richard's, *à la fin*, meaning 'to the end', has no heraldic significance.

Some time towards the end of the fourteenth century, King Charles V of France simplified the arms of France by reducing the number of fleurs-de-lys to three. When King Henry IV, who was still styled King of France and still bore the French arms, had a new great seal struck in 1405, the arms of France were altered so as to correspond to the coat as used by the ruling kings of France. The picture of Henry V's arms depicts the new version of the French arms and also includes what became the royal motto *Dieu et mon droit*, meaning 'God and my right'. Two imaginary supporters have been added in the form of the lion of England and Henry's antelope badge. Yes, that strange creature is what the early herald painters thought an antelope looked like! The royal crest is a little different from that in the illustration of Richard II's arms, as it varied in detail slightly from the reign of Edward III until that of Henry VIII, who used a crowned lion standing on a royal crown; this crest has remained unaltered from that time to the present day.

All the kings from Henry IV until Henry VII used the same arms. Indeed, Henry VII did not so much alter as augment the arms because the supporters he used, the dragon and the greyhound, may be regarded as part of his coat of arms; they were more than just an artistic conceit. Henry VIII usually preferred a crowned lion to a greyhound and these supporters were used thereafter. The illustration shows a simplified version of his arms, the royal crown, now an arched crown, replacing the helm and crest. The wreath of green and white, the Tudor livery colours, environing the shield, is purely decorative but the motto is that which both Henry and his father used, and which has been used by almost every other monarch until the present day.

It is not always appreciated that Mary I's husband, Philip of Spain, was King of England, although he was never actually crowned. After the marriage the royal arms showed half Philip's coat on one side of the shield and Mary's entire royal arms on the other. The shield was supported by Philip's eagle and Mary's lion. Round the shield was placed a representation of the garter of the Order of the Garter. From the end of the fifteenth century the sovereign and knights of the Order, founded by Edward III, customarily environed their arms with the insignia of this, one of the greatest orders of chivalry in the world.

Queen Elizabeth loved gold and it was she who altered the colour of the royal mantling, making it gold rather than red. It continued to be shown lined with ermine. She also gilded the dragon supporter and affected a golden barred helm facing the front. Subsequent monarchs have continued to use the golden helm and mantle.

The Stuart Arms

When James VI of Scotland succeeded as James I of England, the first major alteration in the royal arms for over two hundred and fifty years occurred. To show that he was king of Scotland he needed to incorporate the royal arms of Scotland, the red lion within a double tressure flory counterflory (the illustration **32** shows what this heraldic device looks like). To do this he divided the royal shield into four and placed the royal arms of his predecessors, kings and queens of England and France, in the first and last quarters, the arms of Scotland in the second quarter and in the third he placed a coat for Ireland. King Henry VIII had raised Ireland from a lordship to a kingdom but he never adopted a coat of arms to represent his new kingdom. As a harp badge had been associated

[26]

with Ireland, James adopted a gold harp with silver strings on a blue background. This coat continues to represent that part of Ireland which is still ruled over by the Queen. James also dismissed the dragon supporter, replacing it by one of the two unicorns which supported the arms of Scotland. At the foot of the picture of the arms are two of James's badges, the crowned Tudor rose conjoined to a thistle, symbolising the coming together of the two crowns on one head and the crowned harp for Ireland.

William III and Mary II came to the throne as joint sovereigns, but they used a single royal arms. This was the same coat as that used by their Stuart predecessors, James I, Charles I, Charles II and James II, but, because William was Prince of Orange, Count of Nassau and Statholder in Holland, his foreign suzerainty was demonstrated in the royal arms by placing over the quarterings a small shield emblazoned with the arms of Nassau, a blue shield strewn with gold *billets* (little oblong rectangles) and with a golden lion over all. When William died in 1702 and Mary's sister Anne came to the throne she did not succeed to the Dutch territories and so dropped the arms of Nassau from her royal coat.

In 1707 the Act of Union with Scotland established a single United Kingdom with two legal systems, but one parliament, the Scots sending representative peers to Westminster. On the face of it this seems a rather unfair disposition as many Scottish peers, although they voted at elections for representative peers, could not themselves sit at Westminster. This situation was corrected by the Peerage Act 1963 which gave all Scottish peers a seat and vote in the House of Lords and also extended membership of the House to peeresses in their own right, the majority of which are Scottish.

To symbolise this major constitutional change the royal arms were again altered. As a husband and wife display their marital arms by placing them side by side on a single shield, so the arms of England and Scotland were shown like a marital coat in the first and last quarters of the royal shield. France remained in the second and Ireland in the third quarter. Queen Anne, like Queen Elizabeth I, used *Semper eadem* as her motto in place of *Dieu et mon droit*.

[27]

The Hanovarian Arms

This new arrangement of the royal arms was short-lived as Anne died in 1714 and was succeeded, under the terms of the Act of Settlement, by her cousin George of Hanover, Duke of Brunswick and Luneburg. To symbolise his German dominions, George removed the repeated arms of England and Scotland from the fourth quarter and replaced them by three coats *tierced in pairle reversed*. This sounds obtuse and complicated, but it only means that the quartering was divided in the form of an inverted Y, two coats being placed in the top divisions (the two gold lions passant guardant on red of Brunswick and the blue lion on a golden field strewn with little red hearts of Luneburg) and a single coat in the bottom division consisting of the white horse of Hanover on a red field. In the centre of the quartering a little red shield emblazoned with a representation of the Crown of Charlemagne in gold proclaimed the fact that George held the purely honorary office of Archtreasurer of the Holy Roman Empire. George reverted to the old royal motto which was thereafter used by all succeeding sovereigns.

The royal arms remained undisturbed until 1801 when the Act of Union with Ireland, by which Ireland as a separate kingdom with its own parliament was abolished, argued a change in the royal style and in the royal arms. In 1801 Napoleon was first Consul of the French Republic and was waging war against the British, so it seemed an opportune and apt moment for the king to drop his claim to be King of France. The incipit of the royal style was altered from 'By the Grace of God King of Great Britain, France and Ireland' to 'By the Grace of God King of Great Britain' and the lilies of France disappeared from the royal arms. England now occupied the whole of the first and fourth quarters, Scotland the second quarter and Ireland the third. The German quartering was displayed on a shield placed over the British quarterings and, as Hanover was an Electorate, which meant that George III was technically one of those who elected the Holy Roman Emperor, an electoral bonnet of crimson velvet turned up with ermine was placed over the shield of the German arms.

In 1815, the Holy Roman Empire was abolished under the terms of the Congress of Vienna and the Electorate of Hanover became an independent kingdom. To symbolise the change in its constitution the electoral bonnet gave way to a royal crown.

When William IV died in 1837 he was succeeded by Victoria, the only daughter and heir of his next brother, the late Duke of Kent. But Victoria could not succeed to the throne of Hanover, as what is called the salic law obtained in that country. This simply meant that a woman could not succeed to the throne of Hanover: this passed instead to the nearest male heir, in this case Ernest, Duke of Cumberland.

Obviously, it would have been wrong for Victoria to have continued to sport the German quarterings and so the crowned inner shield was dropped from the royal arms, leaving them as they are today.

The Royal Arms in Scotland and Wales

When the Court is in Scotland an observant person will notice that the royal arms, which are shown at the head of the Court Circular, published in certain newspapers, are different. Upon close examination it will be seen that the royal arms of Scotland have replaced those of England in the first and fourth quarters and that the arms of England have been relegated to the second quarter, Ireland remaining safe in the third. Also, the crest is different. The crowned lion statant guardant has given way to a crowned lion sejeant affronty, that is sitting upright and facing the front, holding a sword in his right and a sceptre in his left paw; over his head is the motto, *In defens*. On either side of the shield the supporters have changed places and are slightly different, in that the unicorn has a royal crown on its head and supports a banner of the cross of St Andrew, whilst the English lion holds a similar banner but displaying the cross of St George. The collar of the Order of the Thistle environs the shield and beneath it is the motto, *Nemo me impune lacessit*. These are the royal arms as used on the Scottish Great Seal and, by custom, also used to represent the sovereign in Scotland on 'By Appointment' signs, the tabards of the Scottish heralds and elsewhere.

But what of Wales? The constitutional position of Wales is different from that of Ireland and Scotland, for the sovereign was never king of Wales. Constitutionally Wales became part of the kingdom of England in 1302 under the terms of the Statute of Wales but Edward I made Wales a titular principality and in 1307 his son Edward was created the first

Prince of Wales and was probably so invested in open Parliament at Lincoln. Wales and the Earldom of Chester became his apanage and from them the prince derived revenues, but he was in no sense an independent ruler. It would have invited disaster for the king to have given his son and heir apparent an independent, strategically placed principality on, as it were, the back doorstep, as there was seldom much love lost between the sovereigns and their heirs, who not unnaturally eyed the throne on which they would one day sit, with unfeigned interest.

The native Welsh Princes of Gwynedd, or North Wales, had been recognised by the English Crown as Princes of all Wales in the thirteenth century. The coat of arms of these princes consisted of a shield divided into four quarters, the first and fourth gold, the second and third, red, with in each quarter a lion passant guardant, alternately red on the gold and gold on the red.

The English Princes of Wales never used these most attractive arms. This is probably because the English attitude to Wales was at the best insensitive and at the worst downright cavalier. When stirrings of unrest in Wales led to the emergence of a dormant Welsh nationalism, the government had to sit up and take notice. Until 1617, when the sovereign created his eldest son Prince of Wales and Earl of Chester, this had been done formally and in open parliament at Westminster. Thereafter, the ceremony of investiture was dropped. Princes of Wales were created, often whilst infants, simply by the issue of Letters Patent under the Great Seal. The princes took no interest in Wales, regarding the title as no more than a title. Even the historic assocation with Wales seems to have left them unmoved.

Towards the end of Queen Victoria's reign, the Bishop of St Asaph conceived a plan for reviving the ceremony of investiture, making it a public occasion and so really associating the Prince with his principality. This excellent idea was not implemented by King Edward VII when he came to the throne but was revived by Mr David Lloyd-George after the accession of King George V. The result was the investiture of King George's son, Edward, as Prince of Wales at a great public ceremony in Caernarvon Castle in 1911.

This closer association of the Prince of Wales with Wales was also symbolised armorially and Edward was assigned the arms of the old

The Arms of HRH The Prince of Wales

princes of North Wales as an addition or augmentation to his royal arms. The heir apparent bears the same arms as the sovereign, except that the royal crown is everywhere replaced by the heir apparent's crown (similar to the royal crown, but with a single arch) and to the arms, crest and each supporter is added a silver label of three points. This looks rather like a comb with three teeth. The old Welsh arms were shown on a shield placed in the centre of the royal shield and ensigned by the prince's crown.

The precedent of the 1911 investiture was followed in 1969, when Prince Charles was invested as Prince of Wales, having been so created on 26 July 1968. In the same year he, like his great-uncle, was assigned arms augmented with the crowned Welsh coat.

I have stated that the shield of the Princes of Gwynedd contained four lions and the question may well be asked, what of the Welsh dragon? The answer is that the dragon is a badge, not a coat of arms.

Some of the many royal badges are illustrated and it will be seen that both the sovereign and the Prince of Wales have dragon badges. That used by the Queen was adopted in 1953, it superceded and augmented the simple dragon badge previously used. It will be seen that the badge is now shown on a shield and so looks like a coat of arms. This was no accident. At the time the badge was adopted there was no Prince of Wales to bear the arms of the Welsh princes and Wales, being part of the old kingdom of England, was not separately represented in the royal arms. This caused a certain amount of ill-feeling and so the Queen was advised to assume a badge which looked like a coat of arms. The Queen, as the fount of all honour, can do what she pleases, but it is rather sad that she should have been advised to break the normal rules of heraldry in order to practise what the knowledgeable might construe as a mild deception on her Welsh subjects.

Commonwealth Arms

It has often been mooted that the royal arms as borne today are illogical, in that they contain the devices of former kingdoms but nothing to represent countries of which the Queen is now sovereign. Where are the arms of the Queen of Australia, or the Queen of Canada or the Queen of New Zealand? The answer is partly historical, partly political and partly practical.

Historically the Commonwealth kingdoms have evolved from independent countries within the Commonwealth, which in turn were originally colonies or groups of colonies. The governments of these colonies and countries were assigned arms by the Crown and these naturally have strong historical and sentimental associations.

Politically, the various countries within the Commonwealth have developed in different ways from quite distinct historical backgrounds and it has seemed wisest to let the countries themselves decide how they would like to be represented armorially. None has seemed anxious for the Queen to bear a single multi-quartered coat of arms throughout the Commonwealth, with each country represented by an individual quartering. Thus, in Canada, the Queen's royal arms are as in Great Britain, but with France in the fourth quarter and three maple leaves in a division at the foot of the shield. In Australia each of the states is represented by a quartering, but all are contained within an ermine border. New Zealand has a single coat symbolising various national features and Kenya bears arms upon an African war-shield.

Practically, it would be impossible for the royal arms to symbolise all the Commonwealth countries, as the post-war Commonwealth is such a very volatile association of countries, that their comings and goings would mean that the royal arms would never remain the same from one year's end to another. The instability of such a situation would only be matched by the expense of constant change. So it seems best to leave well alone and let the royal arms, which have now remained unaltered since 1837, be regarded as a permanent symbol of the stability and authority of the Crown as the dispenser of justice, the guardian of liberty and the only real hope of stability and continuity in times to come.

[33]

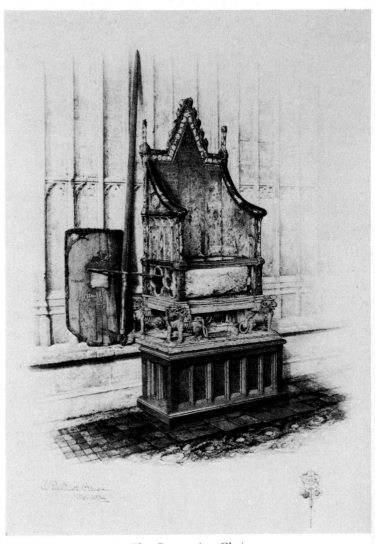

The Coronation Chair

3

THE REGALIA

In 1296 King Edward I, fresh from the Welsh wars, marched to Scotland, captured Berwick, defeated the Scots army and made a grand progress through Scotland to receive the submission of the Scottish chiefs. On this occasion he removed the Stone of Destiny, on which the Scots kings sat at their consecration, from Scone Abbey and brought it south. Although Scotland was to regain her freedom under Robert Bruce, the Stone of Scone was to remain in England, except for a brief holiday in Arbroath Abbey in 1951, whence it was temporarily removed by a group of Scottish Nationalists.

Edward planned to incorporate the Stone in a bronze throne, but later changed his mind and an oak chair was made at a cost of a hundred shillings and the Stone was placed beneath the seat.

Edward II sat on this chair in Westminster Abbey at his consecration in 1308 and it has remained there ever since, except when it was removed to Westminster Hall for Cromwell to sit on at his installation as Lord Protector, and when it was evacuated to Gloucester Cathedral during the last world war.

It seems rather ungracious of the English to have retained the Stone of Scone. However, since the union with Scotland in 1707, the Coronation Chair with the stone beneath it has acquired an added and proper symbolism, because on it the monarch is consecrated sovereign of all Great Britain, not just the southern part of it. Although not strictly speaking part of the regalia, the Coronation Chair is so much part and parcel of the rite of consecration that mention of it has to be made.

I have deliberately referred to consecration because this is the most ancient and important part of what is generally thought of as the coronation ceremony. Really, coronation means crowning, which solemn act forms only part of the ceremony, although it certainly constitutes the most dramatic moment.

The crown with which the Archbishop of Canterbury performs the rite of coronation is known as St Edward's Crown, and it is this crown, in stylised form, which is used to symbolise the monarch, whether depicted on its own, or as part of the royal coat of arms.

It was made, as was most of the regalia, by Robert Vyner, goldsmith to King Charles II, for his coronation in 1661. Much of the old regalia had been seized by Henry Marten by order of the Cromwellian Parliament and eventually was 'totallie broken and defaced' and turned into coin. Fortunately, Sir Henry Mildmay, the Keeper of the Jewel House, managed to salvage some of the richest jewels and bought the rest 'at an easie rate'.

The Crown is made entirely of gold, bedight with precious stones, but the really magnificent jewels are those which adorn the Imperial State Crown. This crown is that which the sovereign wears at the State Opening of Parliament and also at the close of the coronation ceremony, the St Edward's Crown being too heavy to be worn for long. It is true to say that St Edward's Crown is the symbolic crown of kingship, but is itself symbolised and represented by the Imperial State Crown.

Vyner made an alternative crown for Charles II, but it was despoiled of its jewels in 1838 when Messrs Rundell and Bridge incorporated the gems in a new crown made for Queen Victoria. This is the magnificent Imperial State Crown used by the Queen today. In basic form it is similar to the crown it represents, having four crosses formy and four fleurs-de-lys alternately set about the rim. From the crosses rise two arches topped by an orb, ensigned by another cross formy. The crown is far more elegant than the St Edward's Crown, the rim being of open-work silver, rather than solid gold, and it is a mass of precious stones. The most prominent stone, set in the centre of the cross in the front of the crown is the Black Prince's ruby. This stone was given to Edward Prince of Wales, the Black Prince, by Pedro the Cruel in 1367 and is supposed to have been worn by King Henry V in his helmet at the battle of Agincourt. Below the ruby, in the circlet of the crown, is the second largest portion of the famous Star of Africa, or Cullinan diamond, the greatest portion being in the Sceptre with the Cross. This diamond was placed in the crown for King George V's coronation in 1911, replacing the Stuart sapphire which now adorns the cross over the orb. It is called the Stuart sapphire because it was taken by James II when he abdicated and was eventually inherited by Henry, Cardinal of York, younger brother of Bonnie Prince Charlie and the last of the Stuart dynasty. Although the cardinal had a closer heir than George III, he magnanimously bequeathed the sapphire to him and so it was re-united with the other crown jewels. Beneath the intersection of the arches hang four large ovoid pearls, said to have been the ear rings of Queen Elizabeth I.

The orb and two sceptres, which are handed to the sovereign before the actual coronation, were also made by Vyner. The orb is a golden globe ensigned by a jewelled cross, symbolising the belief that 'the whole world is subject to the Power and Empire of Christ our Redeemer'.

The two sceptres are the Sceptre with the Cross, symbolising royal power and justice and the Sceptre with the Dove, signifying equity and mercy. The dove, of course, typifies the Holy Ghost. The Sceptre with the Cross is a particularly beautiful piece, having the largest portion of the great Star of Africa diamond fixed above the rod in such a way that it can be removed and worn separately. Above the diamond is an orb fashioned out of a single amethyst, the cross above it being set with jewels.

Vyner also made the gold spurs with which the sovereign's heels are touched, symbolising knighthood and chivalry. They are sometimes called St George's spurs, as St George, patron of that most noble order of chivalry, the Order of the Garter, is, by inference, the patron and type of English chivalry.

Emblems of sovereignty once used at coronations but discontinued before the coronation of Charles I were the bracelets, being referred to as the bracelets of sincerity and wisdom. They are known as the armills from the Latin word *armilla* meaning bracelet. They were put on the sovereign's wrists before he was invested with the royal stole, a long band of material placed about the neck. At Charles I's coronation, no armills were used, but the rubric read 'Then is the Armill put about his neck and tied to the boughts of his armes, the Archbishop saying:

[37]

"Receive the Bracelets of sinceritie and wisdom as a token of God's embracing".' Thereafter, the reference to the bracelets was dropped, but the stole was still referred to as the armill. This obviously ambiguous description of the priestly stole or scarf continued until the coronation of the present Queen. On this occasion, the rubric stated that the Archbishop shall first put the armills on the Queen's wrists and then shall the Dean of Westminster, assisted by the Mistress of the Robes, put upon the Queen the Stole Royal and Robe Royal.

The armills used in 1953 were specially made by the Crown Jewellers in pure gold, lined with red velvet. They are quite plain except for two narrow bands of decorative engraving and a single Tudor rose which forms the clasp. They were presented to the Queen by her Governments and that of Southern Rhodesia. This was the happy idea of Mr (now Sir) Robert Menzies, then Prime Minister of Australia.

The ring, which symbolises the marriage of the sovereign to the country and consequently is often called 'The Wedding Ring of England' was made for King William IV and is composed of a large sapphire set with four rubies in the form of a cross and surrounded by diamonds. It recalls the red cross of St George, the emblem of England.

Also forming part of the regalia and used in the coronation ceremony or carried in the procession are St Edward's Staff, the Jewelled Sword of State, the Great Sword of State, the Swords of Justice to the Spirituality and of Justice to the Temporality and the Sword of Mercy.

St Edward's Staff is a virge of gold, just over four feet seven inches long and tipped with steel. At one time the sovereign was handed this staff at the entrance to the Abbey to guide him to the place of coronation. Today, it is carried before the sovereign as a symbol of its original purpose. The staff which was made in 1661 is surmounted by an orb, originally said to contain a relic of the true cross.

The jewelled Sword of State is offered to the Church by the sovereign during the service. It was made for King George IV at the cost of £6,000 and is richly encrusted with jewels set in designs which form the rose, thistle and shamrock badges of England, Scotland and Ireland. It is always acclaimed as quite the most valuable sword in the world.

This sword, which is only used in the coronation ceremony, should not be confused with the great Sword of State. This is a hefty weapon, encased in a scabbard of crimson velvet ornamented with the royal arms and with the rose, thistle, harp, portcullis and fleur-de-lys badges. It is a two-handed sword with a blade thirty-two inches long and is the sovereign's personal sword and the emblem of his authority. It is carried not only at coronations but also at the State Opening of Parliament. Because of its length and weight he who carries it has to use a sling to help him support it.

The two swords, carried in the coronation procession as symbols of royal justice to the spirituality and the temporality are identical to all intents and purposes, as, indeed, should be justice meted out to all men regardless of their estate. But justice is not inflexible; mercy too is the prerogative of the crown and this mercy is symbolised by a sword with the point cut off. This is the Sword of Mercy, or 'curtana' as it is usually called. This sword first appears in a coronation ceremony in 1236 when Queen Eleanor, wife of King Henry III was crowned.

Also regarded as part of the regalia are the heavy, ornate gilt maces carried by the Serjeants at Arms at coronations and State Openings of Parliament. These, like the Great Sword of State, are emblems of royal authority. The maces used today, although similar, are not identical as they have been made at various times, the earliest dating from the coronation of Charles II in 1661. They are made of silver gilt and consist of long ornamental staves surmounted by open-work 'bowls' ornamented with armorial bearings and other embellishments. These in turn are ensigned by arched crowns, representing the royal crown and its authority.

The robes with which the sovereign is invested are also sometimes regarded as part of the regalia. They consist of the *Colobium Sindonis*, the *Super Tunica*, the Robe Royal and the Stole Royal. At one time these were handed down from reign to reign and it was noted in 1649 that the royal vestments were 'very old' and when sold by Parliament only fetched a few shillings. More recently, new vestments have been made for each coronation. The actual robes are more fully described in the chapter on Ceremonials.

As the most sacred and solemn part of the ceremony is the anointing, it is felicitous that the vessel in which the oil for the anointing is kept, possibly formed part of the original regalia, having escaped destruction during the Commonwealth. The vessel, called the Ampulla, is in the form of an eagle with outstretched wings. The oil is poured through the beak into a spoon when it is required. Although the bowl of the spoon was made by Vyner, the handle is about 700 years old.

Coronation of Queens Consort

When the king is married, his wife is usually crowned after the royal coronation. Like the sovereign, she is anointed and is then crowned with a special crown which is made for the purpose. That which was made for Queen Elizabeth the Queen Mother contains the Koh-i-Nor, the greatest diamond in the world, which had also been used in the crowns of the two previous consorts. She also has a ring put on the fourth finger of her right hand and is endowed with two sceptres. Like those of the sovereign, one sceptre is ensigned by an orb and cross and the other by a dove. That with the dove is an elegant ivory rod, embellished with gold and was made for the coronation of Mary of Modena, Queen of King James II.

Although it is usual for a queen consort to be crowned, not every consort has been accorded this honour by her husband. The first consort to be crowned on the same day as her husband was Eleanor of Anjou who, with Henry II, was consecrated at Westminster in 1154. This set a pattern, but not one which was followed invariably.

Only the first two of Henry VIII's six consorts were given the privilege of coronation. Queens Jane Seymour, Katherine Howard, Anne of Cleves and Katherine Parr all had to make do without the formal sacring.

Queen Henrietta Maria, the young wife of Charles I refused to be crowned, on religious grounds. She was a daughter of King Henry IV of France, the Huguenot king who, in 1593, embraced the Catholic faith in order to secure the French throne and whose children by his Italian wife, Marie de Medici were all reared in the catholic faith.

Charles II married Catherine, daughter of King John IV of Portugal, two years after his restoration to the throne in 1660. Charles himself had been crowned King of Scots at Scone in 1651 and King of England at Westminster in 1661, but his wife, a catholic like her mother-in-law, was never crowned.

King George IV succeeded to the throne in 1820 and was crowned

[40]

with considerable pomp and circumstance in 1821. For many years he had been separated from his wife, Caroline, who thereafter spent most of her time abroad, apparently living an unedifying and adulterous life. When George succeeded his blind old father, Caroline was persuaded to return to England by Henry Brougham (later Lord Brougham and Vaux) and Alderman Matthew Wood, referred to by her husband as 'that beast Wood'. She resided with the latter at his house in South Audley Street. George persuaded the Prime Minister, Lord Liverpool, to introduce a bill into Parliament to dissolve his marriage. Although this bill was passed with a small majority in the Lords it was not proceeded with, as it was thought that it would be defeated in the House of Commons. The Queen later accepted an enhanced pension and a house, but, when the coronation drew near, put forward a claim to be crowned. The matter was referred to the Privy Council who advised the King to reject the Queen's claim. On the day of the coronation, the Queen drove to Westminster with Lord Hood, but was refused admission by the doorkeepers and returned to South Audley Street. She died a month later. Although Caroline's morals and behaviour were scarcely what is hoped for in a queen, they were certainly no worse than those of her husband. She was really no more than a rather pathetic pawn in a political skirmish which eventually became inextricably involved with the ambitions and aspirations of Henry Brougham.

4

ROYAL CEREMONIES

People are wont to refer to royal pageantry when what they really mean is royal ceremonial, for pageants are re-enactments of past events, while ceremonies are the very stuff of history.

A ceremony is an ordered and traditional way of marking an important or constitutional event. We are all involved in ceremonial in our daily lives. When a man lifts his hat, removes his glove and shakes a lady's hand he is performing a small ceremony, only it is called good manners rather than a greeting ceremony. The way in which football matches are played is essentially ceremonial. The lining up of the teams, the shaking of hands, the ritualistic behaviour of the crowd is all in the nature of a ceremony.

Ritual and ceremony are so much part and parcel of the history of mankind, being the tramlines of rational behaviour on which the vehicle of civilised society runs, that it is a brave and foolish man who scoffs at the ceremonies of state.

I have begged a question; for what is the difference between a royal ceremony and a state ceremony? The late Duke of Norfolk once defined a state ceremony as one paid for by the state and by and large this is correct. A state ceremony is arranged and stage-managed by the Earl Marshal (an hereditary office held by the Dukes of Norfolk), whereas a royal ceremony is organised by the Lord Chamberlain of the Household.

State ceremonies are of two sorts, occasional and perennial. This is my own definition but it is a convenient one. Perennial ceremonies are the State Opening of Parliament, which usually takes place in late

October or early November, except when there has been a general election at another time of year, and the annual Service of the Order of the Garter, sometimes preceded by the investiture and installation of new knights. This takes place at Windsor on the Monday before Royal Ascot, as the Queen has to be at Windsor at this time. Occasional ceremonies are such rare events as coronations, state funerals and the investiture of a Prince of Wales.

To assist the Earl Marshal in his task of masterminding state ceremonies, he may call upon the royal officers of arms, generally and generically called the heralds. They are his staff officers. Whilst the perennial ceremonies do not greatly tax either the Earl Marshal or the heralds, as they run in predestined grooves, occasional ceremonies can be very demanding and can involve a large proportion of the thirteen heralds.

The Coronation

The most demanding, most complex and by far the most important ceremony of state is the coronation of a sovereign. I was privileged, although not then a herald, to be on the Earl Marshal's ceremonial staff for the coronation of the Queen in 1953, and to take part in the ceremony as a special Gold Staff Officer. I hope that I may therefore be forgiven if I give a brief eye-witness account of the coronation and some of the arrangements made for it.

Nine months before the event the Earl Marshal moved into 14 Belgrave Square, London, which the Ministry of Works, as it was then known, had equipped and put at his disposal. The Earl Marshal's chief administrative officer was Sir George Bellew, then Garter King of Arms, the title of the principal herald of all England. Other officers of arms looked after or assisted with the various departments in the coronation office, their number being augmented where necessary by outside help.

The Earl Marshal was responsible for the entire ceremony, other than the actual liturgy, which was the care of the Archbishop of Canterbury. He it was who, at the Queen's command, sent out summonses and invitations to attend, arranged the seating and appointed the ushers, known as Gold Staff Officers. He also issued dress regulations. All these activities, as well as running an efficient press office, took place in Belgrave Square.

The preparation of Westminster Abbey, where the coronation of sovereigns traditionally takes place, and the erection of stands along the route and all matters incidental to these functions, such as seeing that those Gold Staff Officers who came on duty at 6 a.m. were given a good breakfast, were undertaken by the Ministry of Works. Obviously there was always the closest liaison between the Earl Marshal's office, the Archbishop of Canterbury's office and the Ministry of Works; as there was with the Queen's private secretary, who saw to Her Majesty's personal arrangements. The police, armed services and others concerned in the preparations for the outside procession to and from the Abbey also worked in close co-operation with the Earl Marshal's office.

I was fortunate in that my own duties were principally concerned with the ceremonial which, when all is said and done, is the essential part of the solemn, religious, constitutional act about which all else revolves.

At the outset we were faced with a singular problem, as there was only one precedent for the coronation of a queen regnant with a living consort and that was the coronation of Queen Anne. When she was crowned on St George's Day 1702 she was already married to Prince George of Denmark, Duke of Cumberland. Although the records of some coronations are very full and detailed, Queen Anne's was not one of these. All we could find was a slender manuscript account of the ceremony which more or less ignored the poor Prince. However, it proved a sufficient guide for the basic planning of the ceremony, as much of what was to take place was already sanctified by centuries of tradition going back to the days of St Dunstan who, using earlier services as guide lines, composed the elaborate rite used for the coronation of King Edgar at Bath in 973.

St Dunstan's *ordo*, as it is called, grafted onto certain pagan customs, like the giving of symbols and the enthronement, the Christian element of anointing and the involvement of the Church in the making of kings. Certain alterations were made to this rite by Archbishop Anselm and again in the early fourteenth century. This last rite, usually referred to as the fourth recension, is to be found in the *Liber Regalis*, which is still in the library at Westminster Abbey.

In 1603 the service was translated into English from the Latin for James I's coronation, but in all other respects it remained as before. It was left to Archbishop Sancroft drastically to prune the coronation rite for the Roman Catholic James II and to Bishop Compton still further to revise it for King William III and Queen Mary II. Since that time minor alterations have been made from time to time but the essential pattern of the ceremony has remained the same.

At the Queen's coronation, after the procession had entered the church, came the Recognition. The sovereign, attended by the Archbishop of Canterbury and the great officers of state and preceded by Garter King of Arms, was presented at the four sides of the theatre, that is the central area of the abbey between the transepts, where much of the ceremony takes place. The Archbishop asked the people at all four sides whether they were willing to do homage and service to 'your undoubted Queen' and they all cried out and acclaimed repeatedly 'God Save Queen Elizabeth'!

After the Recognition she took the coronation oaths which had been slightly altered to detail the various commonwealth countries, which the Queen swore to govern 'according to their respective laws and customs'. Placing her right hand on the gospels she vowed that she would perform and keep the promises she had made. She then kissed the book and signed the oath with a pen given by my own livery company, the Scriveners of London.

The communion service then began and went on until the end of the Creed. The Queen was then divested of her crimson robe and sat in King Edward's Chair for the anointing. Whilst four Knights of the Garter held a rich and very heavy canopy over her, the Archbishop anointed her on the hands, breast and head, blessing and consecrating her in the words of the prayer, 'Queen over the Peoples, whom the Lord thy God hath given thee to rule and govern'.

The canopy was then withdrawn and the Queen was vested with the *Colobium Sindonis*, a form of white alb and the *Supertunica* or close pall of cloth of gold, together with a girdle. This vestment, sometimes called St Edward's mantle, is a form of dalmatic, the vestment worn by deacons, and is often so described.

Now that the Queen had been consecrated and vested she received the regal ornaments. First came the golden spurs which she touched as a symbol of acceptance. At one time the spurs were buckled onto the sovereign's shoes and then at once removed, but this action was abandoned at Queen Anne's coronation, either because it was deemed indelicate or perhaps simply because the Queen's ankles were not her best feature. At the coronations of King George V and VI the king's heels were touched with the spurs but this was not considered appropriate in the case of a woman sovereign.

Next the Queen received her personal sword, which had been laid upon the altar, from the Archbishop, assisted by other bishops. He admonished the Queen to do justice with it and to 'stop the growth of iniquity, protect the holy Church of God, help and defend widows and orphans, restore the things that are gone to decay, maintain the things that are restored, punish and reform what is amiss, and confirm what is in good order'. The Queen was not girded with the sword, as is customary at a king's coronation but simply received it in her hands, then took it and laid it up on the altar, whence it was redeemed for the traditional price of a hundred shillings by the lord who originally carried the Sword of State, which had now been placed behind the screen, in St Edward's Chapel. Thereafter he bore the sword naked before Her Majesty.

The armills or bracelets were then put on the Queen's wrists. Her vesting was completed by having the Robe Royal (a sort of cope) and Stole Royal put on her. She was now attired in what has been described as 'bysshop's gere' symbolic of the divine and priestly nature of kingship.

Then, seated in the coronation chair, she received the Orb, but this was at once returned to the altar as she needed both hands free to hold the two sceptres. The coronation ring was placed on the fourth finger of her right hand and the Sceptre with the Cross and Rod with the Dove, were delivered to her. The climax of this part of the service was now reached, as the Archbishop placed the St Edward's Crown on the Queen's head. On one occasion the crown was nearly put on the wrong way round so, to avoid any possibility of this happening, a small gold star was attached to the front of the velvet cap of the crown.

As the crown touched the Queen's head all the princes, princesses, peers and peeresses put on their coronets, and the kings of arms their crowns; the trumpets sounded and the guns at the Tower of London fired a salute as those in the Abbey cried 'God save the Queen!'

After the Archbishop had pronounced a blessing the Queen went to her throne in the centre of the Theatre and, in the words of the rubic, was 'lifted up into it by the Archbishops and Bishops, and other Peers of the Kingdom'. This reflects the ancient pre-Christian rite of lifting up a new chieftain upon a shield. This custom was known to the Romans and it is recorded that in A.D. 500 King Gunbald of Burgundy was carried to the church on a buckler and tossed into the air, presumably rather like a pancake. Unhappily, like many a pancake, on the third toss he missed the buckler and fell to the ground. Fortunately this potentially hilarious custom never caught on in England but the idea of raising up the anointed into a high place has always been part of the coronation ceremony.

The Queen then received the fealty of the bishops and the homage of the temporal peers. At most coronations until 1902, all the lords spiritual and temporal came individually to do their fealty and homage but this was a very lengthy business and it was decided that, as at coronations since 1902, the senior peers of each degree only should actually ascend the steps, kneel before the Queen and do homage. The rest, removing their coronets, knelt in their places and said the appropriate words. So it was that the Archbishop of Canterbury only did fealty, being followed by the Duke of Edinburgh and the other royal peers doing homage. Next the Duke of Norfolk, the premier duke, did homage, the other dukes kneeling in their places. In like manner the Marquess of Huntley, the senior marquess present, the Earl of Shrewsbury, the premier earl, the Viscount of Arbuthnott, the senior viscount present (Lord Hereford, the premier viscount of England, being unfortunately five months away from his twenty-first birthday and so just under age) and Lord Mowbray, Segrave and Stourton all did homage with the peers of their degree. In fact, Lord Mowbray was the senior baron but not the holder of the senior barony. This was held by a woman, Baroness de Ros, who clearly could not swear to become the Queen's 'liege man of life and limb, and of earthly worship', although possibly this may have to be changed at the next coronation.

After doing homage, the peer who actually knelt before the Queen touched her crown, as being ever ready to support it. Thereafter the royal dukes kissed the Queen's left cheek but the other peers simply kissed her right hand, thus re-enacting what was done at Queen

The Coronation, 2 June 1953, The Duke of Edinburgh doing homage.

Victoria's coronation. Queens Mary I, Elizabeth, Mary II and Anne were all kissed on the cheek, whilst it is said that Edward VI first had his foot and then his cheek kissed. The chronicler Froissart notes that at Richard II's coronation, there 'came the barons, prelates, and all who held anything under him, and with joined hands, as was becoming vassals, swore faith and loyalty and kissed him on the mouth'. He also noted that the king embraced some more fervently than others for 'all were not in his good graces'. Liturgical pundits all seem to agree that the kiss is an essential element of homage but the area kissed seems to be irrelevant. The importance of the osculation is borne out by the fact that at Henry VI's coronation a special Act had to be passed excusing those who should have rendered homage from doing so, as there was an outbreak of plague in 1429 and close contact could have been fatal, especially as the King was only seven years old.

After the homage the Queen descended from her throne, divested herself of the crown, sceptre and rod and went with the Duke of Edinburgh to kneel at faldstools placed before the altar for the communion service. These faldstools were really *prie-dieux* and in the top of one a microphone was concealed. This meant that the Gold Staff Officer who brought it in had to try decorously to connect the plug. When he removed it after the communion he simply snipped the wire with an elegant pair of sécateurs; I think they were gold-plated but my imagination may be running away with me.

The Queen then made her traditional oblation of an altar-cloth or pall and an ingot of gold. There were once two offerings and the nature of the gifts has varied slightly over the centuries. Queen Mary I offered a 'pall of baudekin'. Baudekin was originally an embroidered cloth of great richness, the warp being of gold thread and the woof of silk; later the term comprehended any rich brocade or piece of embroidery. Queen Elizabeth was less generous, simply donating a cloth of red silk. The ingot offered by Edward II was in the form of a king holding a ring and his second oblation was the effigy of a palmer fashioned in gold, with his hand outstretched to receive the ring. Henry VII and Edward VI offered coins to the value of £24 but poor William IV's pockets were empty and he is said to have whispered to the Archbishop of Canterbury 'I haven't got anything; I'll send it to you tomorrow.'

After the communion the Queen resumed her crown, sceptre and rod and retired to her throne, whilst the choir sung the *Gloria*. This was followed by the archiepiscopal blessing and the *Te Deum*.

Thereafter there came what is known as the Recess. The Queen left her throne and delivered up the regalia, which was laid upon the altar. Then, accompanied by various great officers, she retired to be divested of the coronation robes.

Behind the altar a retiring place had been prepared, complete with a chemical lavatory, on which one of the charladies had been discovered enthroned early on the morning of coronation day. Her excuse for her trespass, which the pompous considered *lèse-majesté* at the very least, was that her sin was occasioned solely by feelings of deep devotion and loyalty. In fact it was a form of anterior (it is tempting also to suggest posterior) fetishism, although she would never have understood what that meant. Rightly she was forgiven.

In her retiring room the Queen donned her royal robe of purple velvet. The Imperial Crown, a more comfortable diadem than St Edward's, was placed on her head and then with the sceptre with the cross in her right and the orb in her left hand she joined the great procession to the west door of the Abbey. From thence she was conveyed in the pouring rain back to Buckingham Palace.

That it rained on 2 June 1953 was a great sadness, for stoical as were the thousands who lined the processional route, the great and rare occasion, although not rained off, was severely dampened. But inside the abbey all went with a smoothness and grandeur which we of this generation have come to expect. Under the careful guidance of the late Bernard Marmaduke, Duke of Norfolk, Earl Marshal and Hereditary Marshal of England, our State Ceremonies have become one of the wonders of the modern world. I think that this is partly because the advent of television and motion pictures has demanded meticulous attention to detail in order to present an impeccable image to a cosmic public, but more particularly because the Earl Marshal of the television era turned out to be a magnificent stage manager. I served under the late Duke for twenty-three years and can attest that his attention to and grasp of detail, his real feeling for history and ceremonial and his entirely direct and uncomplicated assessment of every problem made

[51]

him an ideal master of ceremonies. He had little time for the pompous and self-important but all the time in the world for those who, like himself, had a simple, direct and uncomplicated view of life. His authority was absolute but he wielded it with humour, tolerance and understanding.

To attain perfection we had to rehearse the ceremony and several rehearsals, at some of which the Queen was present, were held at Westminster. I well remember the first efforts of the four Knights of the Garter to carry the heavy canopy beneath which the Queen was anointed. One carried his pole between his legs, another had his at an angle of 45°, whilst the pole of a third shook in his trembling hands. The Earl Marshal, accustomed to carrying canopies in religious processions, showed them how it should be done and then sent them off to the nave to practise.

Because of the media the Earl Marshal's task was strenuous but at least he was spared the Coronation Banquet. Until the reign of William IV the procession had formed up in Westminster Hall, which forms part of the Houses of Parliament. From thence it had proceeded to the Abbey and, after the service, had returned to the Hall for the great coronation banquet.

This was a ceremonial feast, but none the less sumptuous for that. The galleries were crowded with spectators, while the sovereign and the nobility tucked in, many of them performing various hereditary offices. For example, the Duke of Norfolk was Chief Butler by virtue of being Earl of Arundel and Lord of the Manor of Keninghall; the Lord of the Manor of Lyston presented a charger of wafers whilst the Duke of Atholl delivered two falcons. Most important of all, the Lord of the Manor of Scrivelsby in Lincolnshire, a manor long held by the Dymoke family, exercised the office of hereditary King's Champion. After the second course he entered the hall ceremoniously on horseback and thrice challenged 'any person, of what degree soever, high or low' who denied the sovereign's right to the crown, to combat with him; in which quarrel he would 'adventure his life against him'. He then flung down his gauntlet.

Those who claim to perform services at a coronation have to make good their claims at a special court called the Court of Claims, which is convened before a coronation. Although many of the claims before this court referred to services performed at the banquet, others did not and so the court continued to sit after 1821; although for reasons of economy, the banquet was discontinued after subsequent coronations.

So it was that before the Queen's coronation the court sat and allowed certain claims. The Earl of Dundee, as hereditary Royal Standard Bearer of Scotland, was accorded the right of bearing the banner of the arms of Scotland and Captain J. L. M. Dymoke, Lord of the Manor of Scrivelsby, was, of grace, allowed to carry the Union Flag as he could no longer perform the duties of the Queen's Champion at the banquet. The claim of the Bishops of Bath and Wells and of Durham 'to support Her Majesty' were allowed, as were those of Lords Hastings and Churston 'to carry the golden spurs'. Various other claims were allowed but that of the Duke of Newcastle 'to present the Queen with a glove for her right hand' by virtue of being Lord of the Manor of Worksop, was not allowed as his estates had been absorbed by a limited company.

The Investiture of the Prince of Wales

Fortunately for Earls Marshal, heralds and other ceremonial officers coronations occur infrequently. Because Queen Victoria reigned for so long neither the 13th nor the 14th Dukes of Norfolk were ever charged with arranging a coronation. But investitures of Princes of Wales are even rarer events. The memory of the investiture of Prince Charles in Caernarvon Castle in 1969 is still green and many people tend to think that such an event is as much part and parcel of state ceremonial as a coronation; in fact this is not the case.

Princes of Wales, like other peers of the realm, are created by Letters Patent under the Great Seal. Until Charles, later King Charles I, was invested as Prince of Wales on 4 November 1616, it had been customary for this brief ceremony to take place in the House of Lords. The occasion was marked by fêtes and feasts but it could hardly be described as a mini-coronation, nor have greatly taxed the energies of the ceremonial officers. But after this investiture the custom was abandoned, the next Prince of Wales, George, son of King George I, simply being created by affixing the Great Seal to the Patent of creation.

The investiture of Prince Edward, son of King George V, at Caernarvon Castle in 1911 was the first investiture of a Prince for nearly three centuries. Although the central ceremony was traditional, there were several innovations. In the first place the constitutional venue for an investiture was in open parliament not in a ruined castle. In the second place the ceremony had never before been embellished by a religious service, as happened in 1911 and lastly, no Prince of Wales had ever been presented to the people, rather as a king is presented at the Recognition before a coronation. In other words, to please the Welsh people, the constitution was partially set aside with the result that what I have already called a mini-coronation was staged. This is not an adverse criticism; far from it. The ceremony in 1911 and that in 1969, which was largely based on the previous investiture, were splendid occasions which gave many people a great deal of pleasure, enhanced the dignity and meaning of the title, and, from a purely selfish viewpoint, gave me and one or two of my brother heralds an exacting but absorbing and fascinating task.

In 1969, because we had to consider the demands of television and the necessity for taking the greatest precautions to ensure security, we slightly altered the 1911 ceremonial, although the changes were not too significant.

The central, constitutional act was the actual investiture. The Queen, being seated on her throne made from Welsh slate, on a dais at one end of the castle, commanded the Earl Marshal to direct Garter King of Arms to summon the Prince. He came in procession from the Chamberlain Tower, which was sited on one side of the castle. He was preceded by heralds and the Secretary of State for Wales and supported by the Lords Davies and Dynevor. Following him were four lords bearing the princely insignia. Lord Lloyd-George of Dwyfor, whose grandfather, the famous Liberal prime minister, had masterminded the 1911 ceremony, carried the sword; Lord Ogmore bore the coronet, Lord Heycock the virge or golden rod, Lord Maelor the ring and Lord Harlech the mantle.

The Prince approached the throne and knelt before his mother whilst the Letters Patent creating Charles Philip Arthur George, Prince of Wales and Earl of Chester, were read first in English and then in Welsh. Whilst Mr George Thomas, the Secretary of State for Wales, was

1. The Coronation of Harold of England depicted on the Bayeux Tapestry.

2. William, Duke of Normandy, orders ships to be built for the invasion of England.

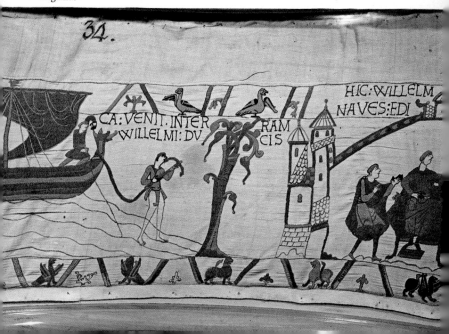

3. King Richard II portrayed venerating the Virgin Mary on the Wilton
Diptych.

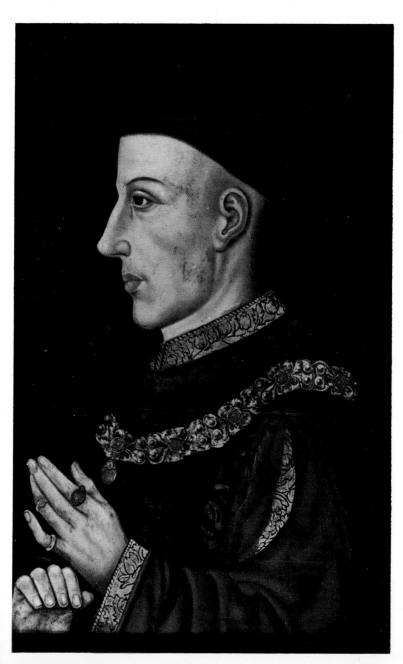

4. King Henry V painted by an unknown artist.

5. King Henry VI painted by an unknown artist.

6. King Edward IV.

RICARDVS · III · ANG · REX

7. King Richard III.

Anno ꝙ o 5 20 octobz imago henrick vii regis illustrissimi
ordinata p hermani rinck Lo regie ... illustrem ·

8. King Henry VII. Portrait attributed to Michael Sittow.

9. King Henry VIII, after Holbein.

ANNO DNI · 1 5 4 4 ·

LADI MARI · DOWGHTER TO
THE MOST · VERTVOVS PRINCE
KINGE HENRI · THE EIGHT

THE AGE OF · XXVIII YERES

10. Queen Mary I painted by Master John.

11. Queen Elizabeth I by Gheeraerts.

12. King James I by Daniel Mytens.

Charles I.ˢᵗ King of
Gr. Britain Fr. & Ireland.
N. 1600. M. 1649.

13. King Charles I, after Van Dyck.

14. King Charles II by the studio of J. M. Wright.

15. King William III, after Sir Peter Lely.

16. Queen Mary II, after William Wissing.

17.   Queen Anne by J. Closterman.

18. King George I by the studio of Sir Godfrey Kneller.

19. King George III.

20. Queen Victoria, after Von Angeli.

21. King Edward VII by Sir Luke Fildes.

22. King George V.

23. King Edward VIII by Frank Salisbury.

24. King George VI by Frank Beresford.

25.   Queen Elizabeth II by Pietro Annigoni.

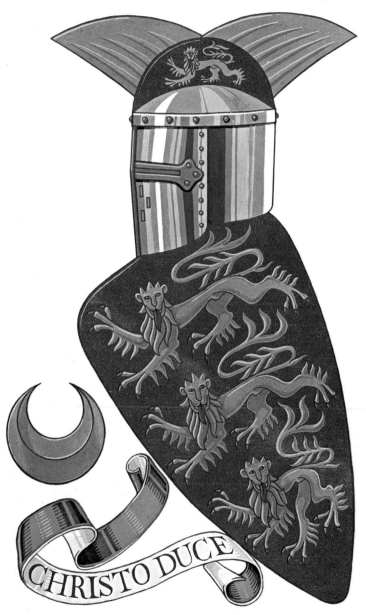

26. Arms of King Richard I.

27. Arms of King Richard II.

28. Arms of King Henry V.

29. Arms of King Henry VIII.

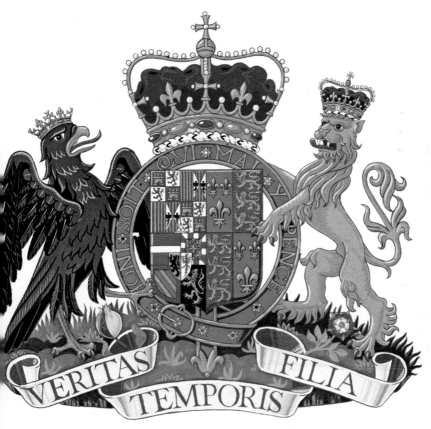

30. Arms of King Philip and Queen Mary I.

31.   Arms of Queen Elizabeth I.

32.   Arms of King James I.

33. Arms of King William III.

34. Arms of Queen Anne.

35.   Arms of King George I, II and III until 1801 with shields of the arms as born
1801–1816 (*top left*) and 1816–1837 (*top right*).

Charles R

Trusty and Welbeloued: Wee greet you well. And
doe hereby Signify vnto you. That vpon due & Serious
Consideration of the Noble & Generous Inclinations of
Our Deare and Naturall Sonns. Charles Fitz-Roy
Earle of Southampton. Henry Fitz-Roy. Earle of
Euston: and of the Lord George Fitz-Roy; Wee
are Graciously pleased to Giue and Assigne vnto them
Respectiuely. Such Armes. Crests. and Supporters, as
euery of them. and their Descendants may & shall
Lawfully beare. and vse on all occasions. And
thereupon. Wee doe Hereby Declare & Ordaine, that
our Said Deare & Naturall Sonn Charles Earle of
Southampton. Shall beare our Royall Armes with
a Baston Sinister Ermine. and for his Crest vpon
Chapeau Gules doubled Ermine. a Lyon Passant
Gardant Or. with a Ducall Coronett Azure. and
Gorged with a Coller Compone Ermine and Azure.
And for his Supporters on the Dexter Side of the
Said Armes. A Lyon Gardant Or. Crowned &c
as is the Crest. And on the Sinister Side a Greyhound Argent Gorged also as is the Lyon with a Coller
Compone Ermine and Azure. And that our Deare
and Naturall Sonn Henry Earle of Euston shall
beare his Royall Armes with a Baston Sinister

36. The grant of Arms by King Charles II to three of his natural sons.

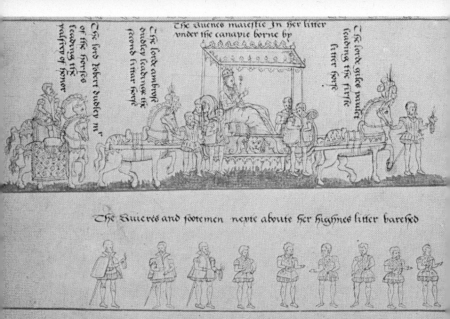

37. (Top) Queen Elizabeth I in her ceremonial litter.
38. (Below) The Queen and the Prince of Wales in the State Coach on their way to the Opening of Parliament.

39.   The Throne in the Robing Room at the Palace of Westminster.

40.   The scene at the Opening of Parliament.

41. The Lord High Chancellor, the Earl of Halsbury, bearing the Purse with the Great Seal. (*Painted by Byam Shaw on the occasion of the Coronation of King Edward VII in 1902: see also following three portraits.*)

42.   The Earl Marshal of England, the Duke of Norfolk, K.G.

43. The Heritable Master of H.M's Household in Scotland, also bearing the Sceptre with the Cross, the Duke of Argyll, K.T.

44. The Lord Great Chamberlain of England, the Marquess of Cholmondeley.

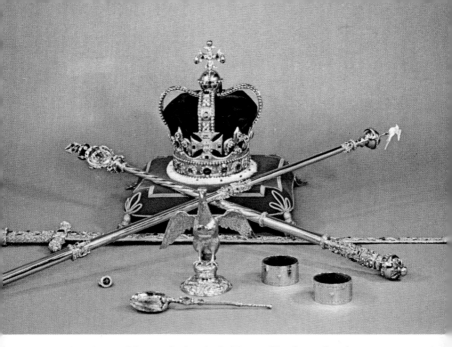

45. A display of some of the Regalia, kept in the Tower of London, and used at the Coronation.
46. Some royal Crowns.

47. The Coronation Coach, which is used only for the Coronation ceremony.

48. Detail of the door panel of the Coronation Coach.

49. In her robes as Sovereign of the Order of the British Empire, The Queen
attends a service at St Paul's Cathedral.

50. The Queen inspects the Guards at the Trooping the Colour ceremony.

51. Trooping the Colour on Horse Guards Parade.

52. The Queen at the Trooping the Colour.

53. Queen Elizabeth, The Queen Mother and the Prince of Wales in the procession to St George's Chapel from Windsor Castle for the Garter service.

54. The Queen presents Colours to the Royal Military Academy, Sandhurst, May 1974.

55.   The funeral of the Duke of Windsor in 1972.

56.   The Queen and Prince Philip with the Duchess of Windsor and Queen
      Elizabeth, The Queen Mother, at the funeral.

57. The scene in Caernarvon Castle at the Investiture of the Prince of Wales in 1969.

58. Prince Charles is invested as Prince of Wales at Caernarvon Castle in 1969.

59. The marriage ceremony of Princess Anne and Captain Mark Phillips.

60. The newly married couple leave Westminster Abbey.

61. The Queen visits Avignon in France, 1972.

62. The Queen inspecting Turkish troops on a visit to the historic First World War battlefield of Gallipoli.

63. The Shah of Iran with the Queen at Ascot Races.

64. The Queen pictured with the Commonwealth Prime Ministers at the Commonwealth Conference, 1968.

65. The Queen opens the New Zealand Parliament during the Royal Tour in 1970.

66. The Queen reading the Address to the New Zealand Parliament.

67. On their visit to Japan in 1975, The Queen and Prince Philip are welcomed at Akasaka Palace at a formal ceremony on their arrival.

68. Prince Philip talks to the puppetmen at the Japanese National Theatre, where traditional Kabuki plays are performed.

69. Royal Garden Party in the grounds of Buckingham Palace.

70. On the occasion of her Silver Wedding, The Queen walks among the people at the Barbican in the City of London and is presented with some violets by a little girl in the crowd.

71. Riding on an elephant during a visit to India.

The Indian locomotive *Prince of Wales*
bedecked for the Royal visit to India for the Imperial Durbar of 1911.

73. One of the Royal helicopters.

74. The Royal Yacht, *Britannia*.

75. Prince Philip competes in the driving event at the Royal Windsor Horse Show.

76. Princess Anne takes a jump at the Burghley Horse Trials.

77. Prince Philip's yacht, *Bloodhound*.

78. The Royal Family watching the events at the Braemar Highland Games.

79. The Queen and Prince Philip on their Silver Wedding.

80. The Queen and Prince Philip with Prince Edward and Prince Andrew at Balmoral.

81. Buckingham Palace with the Victoria Memorial in the foreground.

82. A view of Windsor Castle.

reading the Welsh text the Queen invested the Prince at the appropriate moments. Thus at the words 'and him . . . we do ennoble and invest with the said Principality and Earldom by girting him with a Sword', the Queen suited her actions to the words. Likewise when the wording of the Patent continued, 'by putting a Coronet on his head and a Gold Ring on his finger and also by delivering a Gold Rod into his hand that he may preside there and may direct and defend those parts', he was duly invested with these ornaments. Although there was no mention of the mantle in the Patent this too was put upon him. He next did homage for the principality and earldom and then took his place on a throne provided.

There followed a loyal address to which the Prince replied in what I am assured was really excellent Welsh; it certainly sounded most euphonious to my untutored ear. This exchange preceded an œcumenical religious service.

When this was over the Queen and the Duke of Edinburgh went with the Prince and certain heralds, great officers and members of the Household to present the Prince to the people. To the emotive sound of fanfares of trumpets rising above the acclaim of the people, the Prince was first presented at Queen Eleanor's Gate, then at the King's Gate and finally at the Lower Ward of the Castle. From thence the royal party departed. One way in which the ceremony was lengthened in order to sustain the interest of those in the castle and also that of an estimated four hundred million television viewers, was that the procession into the castle was broken up into a number of small processions. These left Shire Hall Street, where they were marshalled by the heralds and ceremonial officers called Green Staff Officers, at five-minute intervals and walked slowly down Castle Ditch to the Water Gate, where they waited in the Eagle Tower. First came some of the heralds followed by a long procession of representatives of Welsh youth and the peers and gentlemen who were to attend the Prince. The next eight processions all moved through the Eagle Tower and up the length of the castle, taking their places behind the dais. These were the processions of the Corporation of the Royal Borough of Caernarvon, the Gorsedd of Bards, the Lord Mayor of Cardiff, the Mayor of Chester and the mayors of all the boroughs and county boroughs of Wales, accompanied by their suites; of the

Chairmen and Clerks of the Welsh County Councils, the Sheriffs of the Welsh Counties, of Members of Parliament for Welsh constituencies, of peers with Welsh associations and of representatives of the Churches in Wales.

Then peers and gentlemen taking part in the Queen's procession came to the Eagle Tower and the Queen's bodyguards of the Yeomen of the Guard and the Honourable Corps of Gentlemen at Arms entered the castle and took up positions in the Lower and Upper Wards of the castle respectively. Next members of the royal family arrived and then the carriage procession of the Prince himself drew up at the Water Gate. As the Prince entered the castle his personal banner for use in Wales, especially designed for the occasion, was broken over the Eagle Tower.

The Prince's procession formed up in the tower and, followed by the representatives of Welsh Youth moved half way up the castle to the Chamberlain Tower.

Lastly the Queen and her entourage arrived at the castle; the royal procession was marshalled and proceeded slowly to the dais and the ceremony of investiture began.

It was a moving and colourful sight. The splendour of robes and uniforms was set off by the grey stone of the ancient walls and the brilliant green of the sward. It was a wonderful setting for the beautiful singing of the massed choirs, the thrilling fanfares of trumpets and the simple dignity of a ceremony dating back to the reign of the first Edward, over seven hundred and fifty years ago.

A State Funeral

The conduct of funerals was an ancient prerogative of the royal heralds. Anyone who wished to be buried with full heraldic honours had to have his funeral marshalled and arranged by the king of arms in whose heraldic province he died (Clarenceux King of Arms rules South and Norroy and Ulster King of Arms, North of the river Trent). Rules and regulations were laid down by the Earl Marshal and these were carefully observed. Anyone who arranged an heraldic funeral without the licence of the appropriate king of arms was liable to be brought before the High Court of Chivalry to answer for his contempt.

In fact, as the regulations regarding the conduct of funerals have never been rescinded nor altered, a person who wishes to have arms, banners and similar armorial trappings displayed at his funeral must still arrange for it to be marshalled by the heralds. Equally, as the fees have not been raised for some centuries, the heralds might not welcome such a request.

The state funeral accorded to Sir Winston Churchill was a little different. Although the heralds received their ancient fee of £10 each, the ceremony was paid for by the State and the Earl Marshal supervised the arrangements.

Once it has been decided by the sovereign and the government that they would like to offer someone the signal honour of a state funeral, and there have only been eight such solemnities in the last two centuries, there looms the delicate question of asking the deceased-designate whether he wishes to leave the world in so grand a manner. In the case of Sir Winston Churchill the question was put to him by his son at an opportune moment some five years or more before he died. The offer was accepted with alacrity, not to say enthusiasm.

From that moment onward discreet arrangements began to be made for what was known as 'Operation Hope Not'. In an attic in the College of Arms, London, where the heralds have their library and chambers, mourning stationery, plans of St Paul's Cathedral, blank tickets for 'A State Funeral' and similar materials were slowly amassed. Obviously a lot of people knew what was going on. The heralds, officials at the Lord Chamberlain's office, the police, senior officers in the armed forces and many others were 'in the know'. In these circumstances it is hardly surprising that the secret leaked out to the Press but, to its everlasting credit, it held its peace. Not a single newspaper made cheap capital out of the Hope Not story, which speaks volumes for the basic integrity of the Press and of the respect in which Sir Winston was held.

A few days before the great man died those of us who were working on Hope Not were alerted that the end seemed to be near. On the day of his death we were therefore ready to move into quarters prepared for us in the Ministry of Defence. Here two departments of the Earl Marshal's staff were established, one dealing with the ceremonial and the other with seating and invitations.

Although for some years we had been making such arrangements as we decently could, there was nevertheless a vast amount to do in a very short space of time and we worked round the clock in the cause of perfection.

On the day of the funeral, the coffin was borne from Westminster Hall through the streets of London to the great Cathedral Church of St Paul the Apostle, accompanied by ten bands, detachments from the armed forces, chiefs of staff and others. Carried in the procession were banners of the arms of Spencer-Churchill and of the Cinque Ports, of which Sir Winston had been Lord Warden, and four officers of the Queen's Royal Irish Hussars carried Sir Winston's orders and decorations on cushions. Alone in front of the coffin walked the Earl Marshal but only a few of us knew that the master Master of Ceremonies was doing this against medical advice and after taking pain-killing drugs for an affliction of his legs. It was his place, his privilege and his duty to walk and walk he did. Such courage, determination and example would have appealed to Sir Winston.

When the coffin arrived at St Paul's the congregation, including the Queen, members of the royal family and many Heads of State from all over the world, were in their places. The heralds were waiting to receive the coffin. Five pursuivants (a pursuivant is the junior rank of herald) led the procession. They were followed by the officers carrying the orders and decorations and the banners. Then followed nine heralds, of which one carried Sir Winston's spurs, one the crest that had rested above his stall as a Knight of the Garter in St George's Chapel, one his targe (a shield of his armorial bearings especially made for the occasion) and one his sword. Behind the heralds bearing the insignia came the kings of arms, the Earl Marshal, the coffin accompanied by the pall-bearers and the family and principal mourners.

The sombre greys and blacks of mourning apparel were relieved by the dazzling colours of the heralds' tabards, richly emblazoned on front, back and either sleeve with the royal coat of arms, their brilliance only slightly dimmed by the black gauze mourning scarves worn diagonally across them. The use of these sashes was a revival of a custom last observed in 1821 at the funeral of Princess Charlotte, only child of King George IV.

After the service the heralds' duties ended. We all stood on the steps

[122]

of the cathedral to pay a last farewell to the old warrior as his corpse began its final journey through the City of London to Tower Wharf, accompanied by the booming of the guns from St James's Park and the Tower of London. From thence the coffin was taken upstream on the launch *Havengrove* as Royal Air Force aeroplanes flew past in a last salute and the cranes which line the South bank were dipped, as if the very structure of London were bowing to the man who saved it from destruction. From Waterloo Sir Winston was taken to Long Handborough station and from thence to his final resting place at Bladon, hard by Blenheim Palace where he had been born just over ninety years before.

I have dwelt on these occasional ceremonies as it is these which tax the skill of the Earl Marshal and his officers and which mark great and significant occasions in the life of the nation in a way which engraves itself on the memory. Just as a family celebrates such major events in its life as baptisms and weddings with fitting solemnity and rejoicing, so that great family which is the nation does likewise.

The nation, again like a family, also celebrates, though less formally, other annual events. As a family has birthdays and wedding anniversaries, so the nation has the State Opening of Parliament, the annual service of the Order of the Garter and other minor, almost domestic ceremonies, like the distribution of the Maundy Money, the Trooping the Colour and many others.

The State Opening of Parliament

The Earl Marshal and the heralds are only concerned with the first two ceremonies. The State Opening of Parliament is a splendid occasion but because there is little space in the Palace of Westminster, where it takes place, most people only see the Queen and members of the royal family driving to and from the Houses of Parliament suitably escorted.

The Queen arrives at the Royal Entrance to the Palace and is conducted upstairs to the robing room by the great officers of state preceded by the heralds.

Just before half-past eleven the Queen, having put on her royal robe and wearing the Imperial State Crown enters the Royal Gallery. This is a long gallery connecting the robing room with the Princes' Chamber, which is an ante-room to the House of Lords.

[123]

On either side of the Royal Gallery are barriers behind which, on steps specially erected for the occasion, stand the invited guests, crushed like sardines, albeit very contented sardines. At regular intervals in front of the barriers are placed Yeomen of the Guard, looking quite splendid but somewhat obscuring the view of anyone unlucky enough to be standing directly behind one of them.

The heralds, glittering in their tabards, move off at a signal given by Garter King of Arms and lead the royal procession towards the House of Lords. The pursuivants and heralds are followed by various members of Her Majesty's personal household. Behind them are the two junior kings of arms, the Lord High Chancellor carrying his purse, the Lord Privy Seal, Garter King of Arms and the Gentleman Usher of Black Rod. Next comes the Queen, her train supported by two pages and preceded by the Lord Great Chamberlain and the Earl Marshal walking backwards and the Lords carrying the Cap of Maintenance and the Sword of State. Behind Her Majesty are the Mistress of the Robes, two Ladies of the Bedchamber, the Master of the Horse, the Lord Steward, Gold Stick in Waiting and other senior members of the royal household.

The procession winds through the Princes' Chamber, where the Honourable Corps of Gentlemen at Arms is on duty. Here it bifurcates, the heralds and some of the household entering the Lords' Chamber through the left-hand, while the remainder of the procession passes through the right-hand door. As the Queen appears the lights go up and a scintillating scene presents itself. Facing the throne are the judges in their robes and full-bottomed wigs, whilst behind them and on either side are tier upon tier of lords temporal and spiritual in their scarlet parliament robes trimmed with miniver and those peeresses lucky enough to have obtained tickets in the ballot for seats, resplendent in evening dress and tiaras. To the right of the throne sit the heads of mission accredited to the Court of St James in a wonderful variety of uniforms and ceremonial robes, bedight with the flashing stars and vivid ribands of a myriad exotic orders. It is an incomparable and breath-taking scene. Splendour, dignity and tradition mingle to produce an effect and sensation beyond description and unparalleled throughout the world.

The Queen takes her place on the throne, saying 'My Lords, pray be seated'. There is then a long silence whilst the Gentleman Usher of the Black Rod, at Her Majesty's command, signified by a sign from the Lord Great Chamberlain, goes to summon the House of Commons.

The Speaker and members of the Commons eventually arrive (it is quite a long walk) and take their places at the bar of the House. The Lord Chancellor then mounts the steps to the throne, kneels and draws from his purse the Queen's Speech.

This Speech is, of course, not composed by the Queen but is a declaration by the Government of what it hopes to do in the year ahead. Although the literary style, if such it can be called, in which the speech is composed never rises above the pedestrian and commonplace, the content is often surprising and highly controversial. However, dignity is maintained and no sound is heard nor eyebrow raised, manifesting the rise in political blood pressure.

The Speech concluded, the procession re-forms and the Queen is conducted back to the robing room. Here she is divested of her royal ornaments and so returns to her State Carriage. In another carriage the Crown and Sword of State are placed, illuminated by an electric light and displayed in such a manner that those lining the route may see not only the sovereign but also the enduring symbols of sovereignty.

The Garter Service

The Service of the Order of the Garter is very different from the State Opening, being far less formal; more a family affair.

If there are any new knights to be installed these are first invested at a private ceremony in the Throne Room at Windsor on the morning of Garter Day. The knights and officers of the order, in morning dress and wearing their stars, take their places in the Throne Room to receive the Queen and such other royal knights as may be present. These are led in by Garter King of Arms and the Gentleman Usher of the Black Rod, generally referred to simply as Garter and Black Rod.

The Register of the Order, who is a prelate, leads the saying of the Lord's Prayer. Then the knights elect are summoned by Garter and Black Rod. Each new knight, attended by two supporting knights, is then severally brought before the Queen.

First Garter hands the sovereign the blue velvet Garter garnished with gold thread, which she buckles round the knight's left leg. Then Black Rod presents the Riband of the Order which the sovereign places over the new knight's left shoulder. The star, presented to the Queen by the Secretary of the Order, is affixed to his left breast and then the blue velvet Mantle, adorned with the arms and motto of the Order, is presented by Garter. The Queen, assisted by the two supporting knights, places it over the shoulders of the new knight. Finally, she places the Collar of the Order, from which depends an enamelled effigy of St George, the patron saint of the Order, slaying the dragon, over his shoulders. As the knight is invested with these several items the Prelate of the Order and the Register alternately pronounce various admonitions. 'To the honour of God Omnipotent, and in Memorial of the Blessed Martyr, Saint George, tie about thy leg, for thy Renown, this Most Noble Garter.... Wear this Riband, adorned with the image of the Blessed Martyr and Soldier of Christ, Saint George . . . Receive this Robe of heavenly colour, the Livery of this Most Excellent Order, in Augmentation of thine Honour, ennobled with the shield and red Cross of Our Lord.... Wear this Collar about thy Neck, adorned with the image of the Blessed Martyr, Saint George....'

When all the knights elect have been invested each is given a copy of the Gospels which he holds in his upraised hand as the Register administers the oath: 'You being chosen to be of the Honourable Company of the Most Noble Order of the Garter, shall promise and swear, by the Holy Evangelists, by you here touched, that wittingly or willingly you shall not break any statutes of the said Order, or any Article in them contained . . . as farforth as to you belongeth and appertaineth, so God help you, and his Holy Word'. The newly invested knights respond, 'So help me God' and the ceremony is concluded with prayers and a blessing.

The knights all repair to have lunch with the Queen in the Waterloo Chamber. By the time lunch has ended, troops have lined the road from the Castle to St George's Chapel; thousands of spectators have crowded onto the grass and pavements along the processional route and are being entertained by two bands, whilst they check their cameras and perhaps wonder whether they may snap an unmounted trooper of the household cavalry, crashing to the ground, overcome by the heat of the sun on his helmet and breast plate.

Outside the Grand Entrance to the Castle the Military Knights of Windsor and the Yeoman of the Guard are on parade and inside the heralds are being hooked-and-eyed, buttoned and tied into their tabards.

The arrival of the knights and officers of the Order is presaged by a hum of conversation and wafts of cigar smoke. They are swiftly fielded by the tailors who are waiting to dress them in their mantles and plumed hats and then ushered into processional order by the heralds, who then form up in front of them. The Queen and members of the royal family appear and the procession moves off, down the Grand Staircase and through the hall to the Grand Entrance. There the Military Knights and the Yeomen join the procession and lead it by way of the Norman Gate, the Middle and Lower Wards of the Castle and the Gateway of Horseshoe Cloister, to the West Door of the Chapel. The Canons and others of the College of St George meet the procession and lead it up the nave into the choir. As the Sovereign enters a fanfare of trumpets is sounded and everyone catches their breath and comes out in goose pimples; a sure sign that the old magic of state ceremonial is still a living force.

The knights go to their stalls, over which rest models of their crests placed above hanging banners of their armorial bearings. The sovereign instructs Garter and Black Rod to install the new knights by leading them to their stalls; then the service begins.

During the service the Register prays: 'Almighty God. . . . We give thee most humble and hearty thanks for that thou didst put it into the heart of thy servant, King Edward, to found this order of Christian chivalry, and hast preserved and prospered it through the centuries unto this day'. To which all loyal subjects and lovers of the Christian chivalric tradition and the beauty of the ceremony which surrounds it, will say, from the bottom of their hearts, 'Amen'.

The Introduction of Peers into the House of Lords

It is still a facet of the royal prerogative to create peers of the realm. Although today only life peers are so created there is no constitutional objection to the Crown continuing to create hereditary peers. The only reason why this is not done is because the Queen acts upon the advice of her government and no government since the Peerage Act 1963, which enabled the Crown to create peerages for life only, has considered the creation of hereditary dignities to be in the public interest.

What has the creation of peers to do with state ceremonies? Simply that no newly created peer may take his or her seat in the House of Lords unless properly and ceremoniously introduced in conformity with the Standing Orders of the House of Lords.

This ceremony of formal introduction was instituted in 1621. What happens is this. After daily prayers a procession is formed in some convenient room outside the Chamber of the House of Lords. It consists of Black Rod, dressed in Court dress with decorations and carrying his rod, Garter in his tabard carrying his sceptre and the Letters Patent creating the new peer, then the new peer walking in file between two supporting peers of the same degree in the peerage. These all wear their parliament robes and carry cocked hats in their left hands; the new peer also holds his Writ of Summons to parliament. The little procession moves through the Peers' Lobby into the House. Each person in the procession bows seriatim to the Cloth of Estate (that is the throne, which symbolises the royal presence) three times; once at the bar of the House, once at the table and once at the judges' woolsacks. When the procession reaches the Lord Chancellor's woolsack, where he is sitting in his black gown and wearing a full-bottomed wig surmounted by a tricorn hat, the new peer goes down on one knee and presents his Writ of Summons, while Garter presents his Patent to the Lord Chancellor. These the Chancellor touches as a symbol of acceptance and they are then taken to the table, whither all now repair, by the Reading Clerk. At the table the Reading Clerk reads the Patent creating the peerage and the Writ in which the Queen strictly enjoins the new peer 'upon the faith and allegiance by which you are bound to Us' to appear personally in parliament 'to treat and give your counsel ... and this as you regard Us and Our honour and the safety and defence of the said Kingdom and Church ... in nowise do you omit'. The new peer then swears the Oath of Allegiance or, if he has a conscientious objection to taking an oath, he may make an affirmation of loyalty, before signing the Roll. The procession now moves across the house to the spiritual side and then back again to the benches on the temporal side. If the new peer is a baron, as is usual today, he and his supporters will line up in the back bench with Garter facing them so that he can conduct the bowing ceremony.

The reason for this little ceremony is obscure. It consists of the peers sitting, donning their hats, rising, taking off their hats and bowing to the Chancellor, resuming their hats and sitting down again; a procedure which is repeated thrice. Garter then leads the peers down to the floor of the House where Black Rod is waiting to lead the procession out of the Chamber. As the newly introduced peer passes the Lord Chancellor they shake hands and the House acclaims the new peer with the traditional rumble 'Ere rear rear', which is what 'hear hear' sounds like when uttered by members of either house of parliament.

This ceremony, which may be watched from the public galleries, superseded two distinct ceremonies; the investiture of a peer by the king, originally in parliament but later at his palace and the placing of a peer in his seat in the House of Lords by Garter. The investiture ceremony was similar to the investiture of a Prince of Wales, detailed earlier in this chapter and the seating in parliament was not unlike the installation of a knight of the Garter. The 1621 ceremony may well have been devised by Thomas, Earl of Arundel, who had been created Earl Marshal in that year and to whom belonged cognizance of ceremonial matters. Indeed, the Earl Marshal and the Lord Great Chamberlain may both take part in the introduction ceremony should they so wish, although this is something they seldom do.

Trooping the Colour

Why is it that it comes naturally to almost everyone to refer to the 'Trooping of the Colour'? No one complains of having indigestion after 'the eating of an onion'; I can only imagine that there is some affinity with the phrase 'the wearing of the green', and perhaps, too, a good deal of indoctrination by the constant repetition of the error by the press. No, it is the ceremonial trooping the colour of one of the battalions of foot guards which takes place each year to celebrate the sovereign's birthday. It originated in the custom of parading the colour when a regiment provided an escort for a royal prince or commander-in-chief. In the reign of King George IV the colour was trooped or paraded every morning but for the past hundred and fifty years or so one great ceremony has taken place to honour the sovereign's birthday. It is held on Horse Guards Parade before a great concourse of people and is certainly the most colourful military parade of the year.

The Trooping takes place on the Queen's official birthday, not on her actual birthday. The reason for this is that King Edward VII's birthday, unlike his mother's which was in May, was on 9 November and so there was every chance that the weather would be inclement. Edward therefore instituted an offical birthday which was to be a moveable summer feast; in this way warm, if not dry, weather was assured and inconvenient days could be eschewed. Although King George V's birthday was actually in the high summer, he maintained the custom of celebrating an official birthday; a custom which still persists, being marked not only by the parade but also by the issue of a list of awards called the Birthday Honours List.

Some other Ceremonies

The Trooping is only one of many events in the ceremonial year. Another is the November ceremony at the Cenotaph in Whitehall, at which the Queen lays a wreath in memory of the dead of two world wars.

On Maundy Thursday ancient custom prescribed that the sovereign should wash the feet of the poor and distribute alms. Since James II's reign the feet of the poor have remained unwashed, although this ceremony still persists in the Maundy Thursday liturgy of the Roman Catholic Church; however, alms are still disbursed.

Special money, called Maundy Money, is minted each year and the sovereign distributes purses of it to as many poor men and as many poor women as there are years of the sovereign's age. The distribution used to take place at Westminster Abbey but recently the Queen has performed it elsewhere.

A royal ceremony which the sovereign must find very tiring, exacting and perhaps a little boring, but which gives an enormous amount of pleasure, is the conferment of honours.

So many honours are awarded each year, from knighthoods down to the fifth class of the Order of the British Empire, that the Queen has to hold constant investitures. It is enormously to her credit that, unless prevented by absence or illness, in which case another member of the royal family steps in, she still personally confers all honours upon the recipients.

The investitures are held in the ball room at Buckingham Palace, the Queen, attended by members of the Household standing on a dais at one end of the room. Those to be honoured wait in an ante-room whilst a permitted number of guests sit in the ball room. Then, as their names are called, they come forward, bow to the Queen and advance to receive their award. The Queen speaks to each recipient, and usually not just a word of congratulation but some apt and friendly remark which will probably be remembered and become part of the family lore.

It is a great labour of love but I am sure the Queen knows just how much it means to people, particularly the poor and the humble (who need not also be poor), to receive their award from their Queen, to speak with her and to shake her hand. Cynics may turn up their noses at the M.B.E., but to most who receive this relatively modest award it crowns a lifetime of service to their country. This is something the Queen clearly understands and appreciates.

I have come to the point where I have to ask myself, when is a ceremony not a ceremony? Is a royal Garden Party or the drive down the course at Ascot a ceremony or a social function? Perhaps a bit of both for, as I mentioned at the beginning of this chapter, ceremonial is inextricably woven into our lives and this is particularly true of the lives of monarchs, so it is only for convenience that I have touched on the more social ceremonies in the last chapter.

5

SOME ROYAL SIBLINGS

Ever since the reign of Queen Victoria the royal family really has been seen to be a proper family and has been so regarded. Unfortunately the first world war divided that family, as Victoria's eldest daughter and namesake was the mother of the Kaiser and her grandson Leopold became reigning Duke of Saxe-Coburg and Gotha in 1899 on the death of Prince Alfred. This put him on the wrong side of the channel during the first world war. Yet despite the fact that marriage into European royal families necessarily divided the family this made it no different from any other large family. In fact it made it easier for an ordinary family with its quarrels and *mésalliances*, its closeness and its separations, to identify itself with the royal family.

It would therefore be wrong in a book on the monarchy to leave out any mention of the scions of the sovereigns, for several of these have played a noted part in the history of England. Others have a fascination for the historically curious. These latter, which I shall describe in a moment, are less well known and therefore are perhaps more interesting.

The game of historic 'ifs' is amusing, albeit often intensely irritating, for by its very nature it can never be resolved. One series of 'ifs' is that which questions what might have happened if heirs apparent to the throne, who died before succeeding, had lived to wear the crown. Who are these, in most cases, little known royal siblings?

The Young King

It is probably fair to state that after the accession of Henry II in 1154 it was generally assumed, all things being equal, and by this I mean consideration of such factors as age and sanity, that the eldest son of a sovereign would become king on his father's death. When Henry II came to the throne the heir apparent was his eldest son William. Anxious to make certain of the succession Henry held a Council at Wallingford at which the great magnates of the realm promised that they would be faithful to the King's eldest son or, should he predecease his father, to Henry, the second son. In fact William died at the age of four and was buried at Reading near his great-grandfather Henry I, so that his brother Henry became heir-apparent in the year of his birth.

So concerned was Henry II with the question of the succession that in 1170, with the consent of the Great Council, he had his son crowned during his own lifetime. This had been done before on the continent but it was the first and last time it ever happened in England, for it brought nothing but tragedy.

The right of crowning the king belonged to the Primate, the Archbishop of Canterbury. At the time of young Henry's coronation, the Archbishop was his father's implacable enemy, Thomas Becket. Henry would not ask him to crown his son but the Pope refused to permit any other prelate to perform the ceremony. Eventually Henry defied Pope and Archbishop and his son was crowned at Westminster by a selection of bishops convened by Henry. The end of this story is well known. Becket excommunicated the bishops and the King, in a towering rage, is credited with saying 'My subjects are sluggards, men of no spirit, they keep no faith with their lord; they allow me to be made the laughing-stock of a low-born clerk'. At this four knights made their way to Canterbury where they slew the archbishop in his cathedral. In doing this they transformed a holy churchman, albeit also an imperious and implacable politician, into a saint and a saint who was to haunt Henry for the rest of his reign.

It was not long before the Young King began to feel restless, for although he had been crowned, had done homage to the King of France for Anjou and Brittany and been named heir to Normandy, he had been given no real power. Soon young Henry was at war with his brother Richard and eventually both brothers were at war with their father, who reluctantly had to intervene to prevent a full scale civil war. This unhappy situation was resolved by young Henry's death from dysentery. Although his father forgave him, he would not visit him on his death-bed for fear that treachery might lurk even in the heart of the dying man.

His character is a paradox, for against his unforgiveable treason must be weighed his known excellencies. Perhaps a household servant's opinion, as quoted by the chronicler Giraldus Cambrensis, best sums him up. He would give away his last coin to a friend, we are told, and the quality of the knights who followed him for love and without hope of gain could not be equalled; when in arms he was as furious as a wild boar but in peace forgiving and mild.

The Black Prince

The next king to have sons who, because of their premature death, did not succeed their father, was Edward I. John and Henry, his first two sons by Queen Eleanor of Castile and Leon, his first queen, both died in infancy and little is known of his third son Alphonso who died in

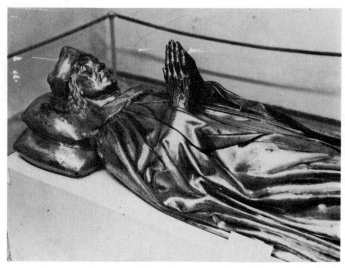

Effigy of Eleanor of Castille, first wife of Edward I

[134]

1284, aged eleven. Edward was therefore succeeded by his fourteenth child but only surviving son Edward.

Edward III's eldest son was also Edward, the redoubtable Black Prince, who became Duke of Cornwall and the first English duke in 1337. This dignity and perhaps more important to the holder of it the attached revenues, was granted to Edward and the first-begotten son of him and his heirs being kings of England. So it is that the sovereign's eldest son becomes Duke of Cornwall at his birth or on the accession of his royal parent. He is not however automatically Prince of Wales and Earl of Chester. The Black Prince was created Earl of Chester when he was two years old but did not become Prince of Wales until 1343. The eldest sons of the monarchs have frequently carried on extensive feuds with their royal sires but Edward was an exception. He was a brave and able commander and constantly fought in the French wars with his father. When only fifteen years old he commanded the van at Crécy and from then on his military career and his unwavering loyalty to his father were exemplary. He was a liberal prince and his generosity was legendary, constantly plunging him into debt. He was a popular hero and it is not without cause that the chronicler Froissart calls him 'the chief flower of chivalry of all the world'.

Alas, the flower withered all too soon and, laid low with dysentery, he 'made a very noble end, remembering God his creator in his heart' in 1376 and in his forty-sixth year. His tomb in Canterbury Cathedral, erected in conformity with instructions contained in his will, is a truly eloquent testimonial to mediaeval craftsmanship. On it appears what he called his badge for peace, the three silver ostrich feathers on a black shield and the motto *Ich dien* (I serve) which many subsequent heirs-apparent to the throne have used, together with the badge known as 'the Prince of Wales's feathers' but which is really the ostrich feathers' badge of the heir-apparent, irrespective of whether or not he were Prince of Wales.

The Black Prince's next brother William died young but Edward's third son, Lionel, Duke of Clarence, was the grandfather of Roger Mortimer, Earl of March, who was named heir by the childless Richard II, the Black Prince's only surviving son. Indeed he was nearest to the throne but it was Edward's fourth son John of Gaunt, Duke of Lancaster, who fathered Richard's successor Henry IV, his fourth but only surviving son.

Prince Edward

The next king who had a son who grew to manhood but never succeeded to the throne was Henry VI. His son Edward, Prince of Wales, was brought up by his mother Margaret of Anjou and was constantly with her, being a pawn, albeit an important one, in the power games played during the Wars of the Roses. Eventually the unfortunate prince, described as 'a goodly feminine and well-featured young gentleman' was either slain at the battle of Tewkesbury or murdered after it, probably the latter, in 1471, being only seventeen years old. Had Henry won Tewkesbury and Edward lived to be king, there might never have been a Tudor dynasty and civil strife might well have continued to dissipate the wealth and manhood of the nation well into the sixteenth century.

Prince Arthur

The birth of Henry VII's son, in whom the roses of York and Lancaster were united—his mother being the daughter of Edward, Duke of York (later King Edward IV)—was a great event. He was given the name of the legendary king and hero Arthur and was carefully nurtured and educated for kingship and, according to his tutor who may well have been biased, he was proficient as a scholar. Arthur is best known to history for his marriage to Katharine, daughter of King Ferdinand V of Aragon and Queen Isabella I of Castile and Leon. The idea of this politically desirable union was conceived when Arthur was only two, the marriage taking place when he was fifteen. Within six months Arthur was dead and his young widow married, for better or worse, her brother-in-law, the future Henry VIII, who had various male children by her, none of which survived infancy.

Prince Henry

Another king whose eldest son was carefully educated and prepared for kingship, was James I. His son Henry Frederick (the first of the royal line to be given two Christian names) was nine years old when, in 1603, his father succeeded to the throne of England. It seems clear that had he lived he might well have altered the course of history. Even in his teens he realised the danger of marriage to a Catholic and it is reasonable to suppose that, grown to manhood, he would have been able to check the disastrous course his father later pursued. But poor Henry died of a fever after a game of tennis in 1612 and his luckless brother Charles became heir-apparent to the throne he was eventually to lose to Cromwell.

Poor Fred

George II's eldest son Frederick Louis, like the Black Prince, died before his father but sired the next king, George III. To say that Frederick and his father did not see eye to eye would be a massive understatement. George II's opinion of his son is eloquently given in the following royal appreciation of the prince: 'My dear first born is the greatest ass, and the greatest liar, and the great *canaille*, and the greatest beast in the whole world and I heartily wish he were out of it'. Frederick, perhaps excusably, responded by setting up his own court and siding with the king's enemies. The royal relationship was an unedifying one. The king's parsimony and the prince's extravagances kept them at arms' length; the prince's popularity was directly related to his father's unpopularity and not to his instrinsic virtues.

Indeed, as Horace Walpole noted, his principal virtue was generosity which was counterbalanced by his insincerity and notorious mendacity. Yet one cannot help wondering whether, if he had been more carefully reared and more generously handled and had survived his father, kingship might not have made the man. As it was the noted epitaph:

> 'Here lies Fred,
> Who was alive and is dead . . .
> There's no more to be said.'

sadly evaluates his place in history.

The Dukes of York and Kent

Queen Victoria only came to the throne because her three uncles, George IV, Frederick, Duke of York and William IV all died without surviving issue and her father—Edward Augustus, Duke of Kent— predeceased her, leaving no other children.

The Dukes of York and Kent were both soldiers. Although the former held the post of Commander-in-Chief of the army for many years he was not a good commander in the field. He was courageous, humane and good-natured but was also woefully inexperienced and his true value was as an enlightened administrator. In his war against favouritism, corruption and political influence in military appointments, he was far more successful than in his disastrous campaigns against the French in the Low Countries.

It was unfortunate that the duke, who opposed corruption, should himself have been caught up in the activities of his notorious mistress Mary Anne Clarke, a scheming lady who was paid money by officers seeking promotion, knowing of her intimacy with the duke.

The duke was exculpated by the House of Commons from any knowledge of the bribes his mistress accepted but his careless behaviour was deprecated. He resigned from being Commander-in-Chief but was reinstated by his brother the Prince Regent two years later. A motion in the House of Commons censuring his reappointment was heavily defeated, thus demonstrating the duke's intrinsic popularity.

Queen Victoria's father, although he did not hold so exalted a military office as his brother, was a keen soldier. Unfortunately he was also a great martinet, which was his undoing. In 1802 he was appointed to command the bored and drunken garrison in Gibraltar. So seriously did he take his duty to restore order and discipline that before long he had a near mutiny on his hands and was recalled home. This he considered an affront and held his brother, the Duke of York, to blame.

This quarrel with his brother and debt, that endemic disease of the Hanoverians, somewhat soured his life but he was not a bad man. Far from it, his virtue in an age of corruption and scandal was remarkable. He was an indefatigable supporter of charities both with money, when he had any, and with his time and energy. He patronised the philanthropist Robert Owen, often hailed as the father of English socialism. Even when many deserted Owen after he had propounded various curious religious beliefs, the duke remained unmoved and wrote to Owen that he was a 'full and devoted convert' to his philosophy 'in principle, spirit and practice'.

The duke married Queen Victoria's mother, Victoria, Princess

Dowager of Leinningen and daughter of Francis Frederick, Duke of Saxe-Coburg, just two years before he died, having for the previous twenty-seven years lived a happy, unmarried life with a certain Madame de St Laurent, a Canadian lady. When, out of a sense of duty, the duke took a wife, his gay and devoted mistress retired to a convent in a truly mediaeval manner.

The Duke of Clarence and Avondale

The last royal sibling who, had he lived, would have been crowned king was Albert Victor Christian Edward, eldest son of Edward, Prince of Wales, later King Edward VII. The prince was born in 1864, was created Duke of Clarence and Avondale and Earl of Athlone in 1890 and died of pneumonia on 14 January 1892, aged twenty-eight. As one born to be king the nation had observed his career and the development of his character with interest and no one had watched more closely than his grandmother, Queen Victoria. That she wrote a moving letter to the Home Secretary thirteen days after his death speaks volumes for the worth and promise of the young prince.

She stated in the letter, which was published in *The Times* on 27 January 1892:

'The overwhelming misfortune of my dearly loved Grandson having been thus suddenly cut off in the flower of his age, full of promise for the future, amiable and gentle, endearing himself to all, renders it hard for his sorely stricken Parents, his dear young Bride, and his fond Grandmother to bow in submission to the inscrutable decrees of Providence'. The Queen goes on to state that she loved him as a son *'whose devotion to me was as great as that of a son'*.

Her reference to his young bride should really have been to his young fiancée, for the prince had recently been betrothed to Princess Mary of Teck. Eighteen months later she married his next brother, George, Duke of York and later King George V.

So much for those who might have been king had not 'the inscrutable decrees of Providence' decided otherwise. Of these only Henry, the Young King, the Black Prince and poor old Fred lived long enough to make their mark on history; what impression the others might have made had they been spared is a matter for even greater speculation.

The Empress Matilda

Other royal siblings occupy more or less of the pages of history according to the power they were able to wield. The kings naturally tried to
keep this power within bounds and harnessed to their own ends as far
as possible.

Perhaps the first post-Conquest royal sibling to send a definite ripple
across the lake of history was a woman, Matilda, only child, after the
death of her brother William, of King Henry I.

She is known to history as the Empress Matilda. This is because she
was married at the age of thirteen to Henry V, the Holy Roman
Emperor. Her husband was thirty years her senior and she found herself
back in England, a widow, aged about twenty-four, in 1125. Her father,
anxious to secure the succession of her line, arranged a new marriage
for her, this time with Geoffrey, Count of Anjou. England had never
had a queen regnant and there was naturally much opposition to the
idea in a bellicose, male-dominated society, but equally there was no
reason why there should not be a queen regnant and Henry determined
that there should be.

Matilda, or Maud as she was called in England, was cast in the right
mould. She was a proud, fearless, scheming woman. She seems to have
been a mediaeval version of Queen Elizabeth I, having 'the nature of
a man in the frame of a woman'.

One of the most important elements in life is timing. To be in the
right place at the right moment gives anyone an advantage over a rival.
So it was when Henry I died on 1 December 1135. His daughter was
in Anjou at the time with her husband but Stephen, a grandson of
William the Conqueror and a claimant to the throne, got to London
first and staked his claim. With the help of his brother Henry, Bishop
of Winchester, the Council was swayed and Stephen was crowned king.
Although Maud, aided by her half-brother Robert, Earl of Gloucester,
tried to wrest the crown from him, she was unsuccessful and England
was plunged into a twilit period of anarchy and devastation. Maud
retired to Anjou and played out her life as a skilful and potent counsellor
to her son Henry, who must have both inherited and acquired from her
many of those qualities which made him one of England's great kings.

The King of the Romans

A grandson of King Henry II, Richard, second son of King John, and Earl of Cornwall, achieved the distinction of being elected King of the Romans in 1257. Unfortunately the electors were dissatisfied at the amount paid them by Richard and, although he had been crowned at Aachen, by the Archbishop of Cologne, they elected Alphonso X of Castile in his place. Richard, who was a wealthy man and a clever financier, returned to England, somewhat poorer, in 1259. He had the qualities of a statesman and, although usually a severe critic and opponent of his brother Henry III, in the last analysis he supported him against de Montfort. Although he married three times, his first two wives being considerable heiresses, and by them had about seven children, he left no descendants. He did however show that there are possibilities open to scions of the royal house beyond the shores of their native land.

John of Gaunt

John of Gaunt, Duke of Lancaster, fourth son of King Edward III and progenitor of the House of Lancaster, assumed the title of King of Castile after marrying Constance, daughter and co-heir of Peter, King of Castile and Leon. When Peter died his evil brother Henry of Trastamare had usurped the throne and John tried, unsuccessfully, to become king not just in name but also in fact. Although John was rich, having first been married to his kinswoman Blanche, daughter and co-heir of Henry, 4th Earl and 1st Duke of Lancaster, who brought him her fortune, he was not a great soldier. In fact, he was not a great politician either but he was an honest, affable man who, during his father's declining years and after the death of his brother the Black Prince, had much power and influence in the land. His life has been romanticised, so that of all Edward's sons, even the Black Prince, he whom Shakespeare calls 'time honoured Lancaster' (actually he was fifty-eight when he died) has become a brighter star in the firmament of history than his merits and achievements really warranted.

More recently Miss Anya Seyton's novel *Katherine* has further glamorised Gaunt with glimpses of life in his famous Savoy Palace and the love story of his association with and eventual marriage to Catherine Swynford, the mother of the famous Beauforts, about whom more details are given in the chapter on royal bastards.

Although Shakespeare's plays are not the places in which to rummage for historical profundities, Gaunt's reply to the Duchess of Gloucester, when asked how she should avenge the murder of her husband Thomas at Richard II's instigation, seems true to character:

> *'God's is the quarrel; for God's substitute,*
> *His deputy anointed in His sight,*
> *Hath caused his death: the which, if wrongfully,*
> *Let Heaven revenge, for I may never lift*
> *An angry arm against His minister.'*

Thomas, Earl of Gloucester

Thomas, Earl of Gloucester, was the seventh of Edward III's notable sons and had, in fact, lifted an angry arm against God's minister in the person of the twenty-year-old King Richard II. He and others had forced the King to banish his unpopular favourites. They had defeated de Vere, the King's principal friend, at the battle of Radcot Bridge in Oxfordshire. The King was at their mercy, which was scant. After some debate the King was spared but his power was assumed by Gloucester and the other four Lords Appellant, as they were called. His friends and supporters were brutally despatched. But Richard was not defeated. He retired and bode his time. Then in May 1389 he took his seat at the Great Council and announced that as he was now of full age he would henceforth rule. Bishop Thomas Arundel surrendered the Great Seal and Richard had accomplished a bloodless *coup*. He ruled wisely and well and did not take revenge upon Gloucester and the other Lords Appellant. They continued to exercise limited power in certain fields and must have been lulled into a sense of false security, for all the while Richard was plotting the subjugation of the barons and parliament, the establishment of absolute monarchy and revenge upon his enemies.

In 1397, almost eight years after his *coup* Richard summoned parliament and struck. Most of his enemies were seized and executed but Gloucester was arrested and taken to Calais by Thomas Mowbray, where he was either strangled or smothered. A sad end to a relatively short life which could have yielded much finer fruit if only Thomas, like John of Gaunt, had been loyal.

The Dukes of Bedford and Gloucester

The Bodleian Library at Oxford is one of the most famous libraries in the country and is known to scholars and bibliophiles the world over. It is named after an Elizabethan scholar and diplomat, Sir Thomas Bodley. When he retired in 1598 he thought that he could not busy himself to better purpose than 'by redusing that place which then in every part laye ruined and wast, to the publique use of studients'. 'That place' was Duke Humphrey's Library, the university library which had been dispersed and destroyed in the reign of King Edward VI, in the belief that many of the works it contained were secular or downright evil.

One of the most magnificent, extant, illuminated manuscripts of the fifteenth century is the Bedford Book of Hours. This superb memorial to the craftsmanship of the age contains over fifty large miniature paintings and more than a thousand smaller ones. It has belonged to many people, being first given to King Henry VI in 1430, but it is now safely preserved in the British Library.

What on earth have the Bodleian Library and the Bedford Book of Hours to do with the royal siblings of England? Simply this: the Duke Humphrey who gave his name to the original library at Oxford and he who commissioned the Bedford Book of Hours were both brothers of King Henry V. Humphrey, Duke of Gloucester, was a book collector who, during the last years of his life, which he spent virtually in retirement, gave his collection of books to Oxford. When in 1444 the university proposed to build a special new library to house them, the duke was prompted to make, as was anticipated, further gifts of books and cash to the university. In gratitude the library was named after him. His brother John, Duke of Bedford, though an able soldier, was also a patron of the arts and his name has been remembered by posterity because of the magnificent book which he and his wife ordered to be written and illuminated as a present for his pious young nephew, King Henry VI.

Although the names of the two dukes have been known to generations of scholars and students of the fine arts, they were more noted in their day as the regents of the kingdom during the minority of Henry VI. Henry V left the France he had subjugated to his son. Everything boded well; Henry's victory at Agincourt had captured the imagination of the masses, rich lands in France lay at the mercy of the English king and two able soldiers and administrators were there to manage this rich inheritance. Unfortunately things did not work out as smoothly as seemed likely. Bedford went to France as Regent and there showed himself an astute governor and skilful general at that difficult period of consolidation which always follows a conquest. But an enemy at once frail and immensely powerful rose up to drive back the English, Joan of Arc. She turned the tide of war until, forsaken by her countrymen and burnt at the stake with Bedford's approval, her sanctified spirit lived on to destroy for ever the dream of a France dominated by England. Four years later Bedford died.

Humphrey of Gloucester was Regent in England where he had to contend with the rivalry of his immensely rich, adroit and powerful half-uncle, Henry Cardinal Beaufort, Bishop of Winchester. He also received the backwash of the reverses suffered in France both before and after the execution of St Joan. He did not add to his popularity by contracting a marriage with Jacqueline, daughter and heiress of William, Duke of Bavaria. The trouble was that the lady was already contracted to a singularly unattractive teenager, John, Duke of Brabant. The Pope refused to annul the first contract and Humphrey consoled himself by marrying her lady-in-waiting and his concubine, Eleanor Cobham, of whose two children he was already the father.

Cardinal Beaufort now struck at his adversary by persecuting his new wife. She was accused of plotting to kill King Henry VI by witchcraft. She was said to have made a wax effigy of him which periodically she put before the fire so that it wasted away, with the intention that the King should wane in like manner. She was tried and sentenced to walk the streets of London for three days, barefoot and in penitential garb and then to be imprisoned for life.

Thus humiliated, with the king approaching the age when he would be assuming the reigns of government himself, Humphrey retired and devoted himself to his cultural interests; learning, books and the great artistic revival known as the Renaissance, which was sweeping through Europe from Italy like a cleansing, or as some would have it, a corrupting flame.

Eventually his enemies arrested him when he appeared at a parliament summoned to meet at St Edmondsbury in 1447. Seventeen days later he 'died' and his unscarred corpse was exhibited to prove that death was due to natural causes, but obviously a clinical examination of the whole body was not made and the smell of murder must always haunt the passing of 'Good Duke Humphrey'.

Richard, Duke of York

The latter part of the fifteenth century was taken up by the civil, dynastic struggle known as the Wars of the Roses. In these many of the royal siblings of the houses of York and Lancaster were naturally deeply embroiled.

Pre-eminent among these princes was Richard, Duke of York, the father of King Edward IV. He was a loyal, virtuous, able, statesmanlike character, and for these very reasons and because he was head of the House of York, the malcontents, and there were many, looked to him as their leader. He served Henry VI faithfully and well, and as Governor in Ireland he did great work, at once subduing the Irish but also winning their respect. When eventually he took up arms it was not against the King but to protect his rights as heir presumptive to the throne against the Beauforts, the legitimated descendants of John of Gaunt by Katherine Swynford and the nearest Lancastrians to the throne. Even on this occasion blood was not shed, diplomacy winning the day. York declared himself the king's liegeman and the king agreed to form 'a sad and substantial Council' of which York was to be a member.

Then came York's finest hour. The King went mad in 1453. Edmund Beaufort, Duke of Somerset and head of his house, was discredited by the losses in France where he was in command. York was made Protector of the realm and, commanding the support of parliament, ruled wisely, with great moderation and generosity to his enemies. All this without pursuing any personal ambition for the throne, as the mad Henry had become the father of a son and heir.

When the King's madness left him as swiftly as it had struck him down, York retired and did not seek to retain power. But once again, with the Beaufort faction back in favour, York was forced once more to march against the King's evil advisers. Blood was shed at St Albans but all York sought was to strengthen and protect the King. It was an uneasy period, for despite York's honourable and patriotic intentions, his followers were forever plotting to depose the King, having an eye to gain the fulfiment of personal ambitions and the settlement of private vendettas. Eventually the two sides met in bloody combat at Wakefield in Yorkshire and Richard, third Duke of York, was slain. So died a really great prince who, had he been more ruthless, might have carved himself a greater niche in history.

George, Duke of Clarence

One of York's sons has been immortalised by Shakespeare, although he only darted like a dragonfly over the pages of history, insubstantial but exotic; this was George, Duke of Clarence. Who does not remember the evil Gloucester, later Richard III, plotting the murder of his brother Clarence by setting him and King Edward IV 'in deadly hate the one against the other'? Then, that night in the Tower, when the first murderer stabs poor George crying—'Take that, and that: If all this will not do, I'll drown you in the malmsey-butt within.' It is certainly true that Clarence was attainted by parliament and his execution left to the King, but whether the popular sixteenth-century legend of the drowning in wine is true will never be known. It is sad, although not perhaps from the poor Duke of Clarence's point of view, that some of the more colourful and dramatic episodes of history remain unfathomable enigmas.

Lady Jane Grey

The style 'Lady' suggests a certain maturity and many people think of Lady Jane Grey as a mature woman, albeit a young one. In fact, if she had lived today, she would have been taking her 'O levels' when she was placed upon the throne by her unscrupulous, unpopular but powerful father-in-law, John Dudley, Duke of Northumberland. Who was Jane and why was she chosen to succeed King Edward VI? She was the grand-daughter of King Henry VIII's younger sister, Mary, wife of Charles Brandon, Duke of Suffolk. Her mother, Frances, who was living when she was made 'Queen', married Henry Grey, first Duke of Suffolk of the Grey family.

When Edward died Northumberland was Lord President of the Council. He calculated that there would be resistance to the next heir, Henry VIII's daughter Mary, because she was a devout Catholic. He therefore felt confident that backed by his power and influence, Jane would win popular support, even although she had no real hereditary claim to the throne.

He strengthened his hand by procuring from the dying King his nomination of Jane as his successor. Jane was proclaimed Queen and taken to the Tower for safety, whilst Northumberland marched against Mary who had fled to East Anglia, insisting that she was the rightful queen. Perhaps because of Northumberland's unpopularity and obvious ambition, because the orderly manner of succession to the throne was being manifestly overturned and perhaps too because the country was not nearly as Protestant as some supposed, Mary commanded a large following. Northumberland capitulated and was executed and Mary became queen. She spared Jane and her husband Guildford until their continued existence menaced her safety. They were executed early in 1554. Jane, then sixteen years old, met her fate with great courage, embracing the Protestant religion and vowing that she had never aspired to the Crown. She died the beautiful, pathetic victim of another's ill-conceived ambition.

The Princes of the Rhine

The immediate relatives of the sovereign were virtually non-existent during the latter half of the seventeenth century, during most of which Elizabeth I, the Virgin Queen, sat on the throne. However, James I was a patriarchal monarch, having seven children by his wife Anne of Denmark. His daughter Elizabeth married Frederick V, Elector Palatine of the Rhine, Duke of Bavaria and later King of Bohemia. He was known as the 'Winter King' as he reigned for so brief a period, being swiftly thrown out, because he was a bigoted Calvinist in an essentially Catholic country. Three of their sons became Knights of the Garter, Rupert,

Maurice, and Edward. All were devoted Royalists and loyal supporters of their uncle King Charles I and of their cousin King Charles II.

Although Prince Maurice distinguished himself in the civil war, Rupert of the Rhine became the popular hero, the leader of the Royalist cavalry. What he lacked in military expertise, and it must be remembered that he was only twenty-three when he commanded the cavalry at the battle of Edgehill, he made up in courage, glamour and *élan*. Rupert was very much to the fore in most of the famous battles of the civil war, his horsemen menacing and usually defeating the Roundheads. He was victorious at Chalgrove Field; Bristol fell to him; he relieved Newark; defeated the Roundheads at Stockport; took Liverpool and suppressed a rising in Wales. As the year 1645 dawned the Royalist cause looked as if it must triumph but the rise of Cromwell, who proved himself to be no mean general, the employment of Scottish troops and the superior artillery of the Roundheads turned the tide of victory into defeat. Rupert was overcome at the battle of Marston Moor and the Royalists were again defeated at Naseby. The bravery, the passion, the ever-increasing military expertise of King Charles and Prince Rupert and their daring offensive tactics, in the end proved no match for the superior numbers and strong artillery of the Roundheads, under their able leader Oliver Cromwell.

Early in 1646 Prince Rupert and Prince Maurice were ordered to leave England. They took to the sea and Maurice was drowned in 1652, during one of his brother's piratical cruises, which eventually ended up in Barbados. Rupert returned to England with Charles II at his restoration in 1660 and pursued his naval career with the English fleet, which he and General Monck commanded in the first war against the Dutch. He also fought in the second Dutch war and thereafter was First Lord of the Admiralty until shortly before his death in 1682. The noble, loyalist, royalist German prince, who had been created Duke of Cumberland and Earl of Holderness by his uncle Charles I, was, quite properly, laid to rest in Westminster Abbey.

The Pretenders

Prince Rupert had served at sea with his cousin James, Duke of York. James succeeded his brother Charles II as King but his own son, James, never came to the throne, which had been offered to James's daughter Mary and her husband William of Orange. The infant James Francis Edward is better known to history as the Chevalier of St George or the Old Pretender.

In 1701 James II died and, to the surprise and consternation of all Englishmen, the French king, Louis XIV, recognised and promised to support his young son as King. There followed what almost amounted to a European war in which the great Duke of Marlborough earned immortality. The war ended with the Treaty of Utrecht in 1713, the death of Queen Anne in the following year and the securing of the Protestant succession in the person of George I.

But all was not well. The Scots were unhappy about the Act of Union, by which the crowns and parliaments of Scotland and England had been united in 1707; the Tories were dissatisfied with George I and his Whig advisers and there was a feeling abroad that the Old Pretender, although unknown in Great Britain, was the rightful heir to the throne. An aura of romance hung about the head of 'the King across the water' and, had the Jacobite cause been more ably managed, the Hanoverians might well have been overthrown.

As it was the 1715 rising was a complete failure. It started in Scotland, where the cause had the strongest support, but the Government at Westminster acted swiftly and surely. Repressive measures were taken; the Duke of Argyll led the Hanoverian forces in Scotland and Lord Derwentwater's Jacobite forces in the North of England were routed by General Carpenter at Preston. All the while the object of the rebellion, the Old Pretender, was nowhere to be seen. He did not land in Scotland until December 1715 when most of the fighting was over. He was crowned at Scone but almost immediately returned to France with some of his followers, abandoning others to their fate upon the block.

The Old Pretender plotted no more rebellions. He was married in 1719 to Princess Clementina Sobieska of Poland and by her he had two sons, Charles and Henry. He resided in Rome, a melancholy, irresolute figure, separated from his wife, mainly because of his licentious ways, and a pensioner of the Pope. His followers deserted him when they realised that he would never make any further effort to regain the throne and champion the Jacobite cause. Instead they switched their hopes and allegiance to his elegant, intelligent and attractive young son, the Bonnie Prince Charlie of history.

In 1745, when England was engaged in wars on the continent, Charles set sail for Britain to win back the throne for his father. He had hoped for French support but in the end he left in a small, hired ship with a few friends. He landed in the Hebrides on 23 July 1745 and about four weeks later he raised his standard at Glenfinnan. He was joined by Lord George Murray, an able soldier, Cameron of Lochiel and others and marched South. At first all went well, but the lack of support from the French and relative indifference of the English, who did not rally to Charles's call to arms as he had hoped, meant that the Jacobite force, though aggressive, was small.

However, Charles evaded the Duke of Cumberland, a son of George II, who had been sent against him with superior forces, and reached Derby. The decision then had to be made as to whether to march on London. In view of Charles's small army and the lack of enthusiasm for his cause, Murray advised him to retire and consolidate his forces in Scotland. This he did but Cumberland caught up with him at Culloden where his army was cut down and dissipated in a terrible holocaust. Cumberland massacred about two hundred prisoners, another hundred being executed, including Lords Lovat, Kilmarnock and Balmerino who are venerated as martyrs by loyal Jacobites. Cumberland's cruelty earned him the approbrium of history and the nickname 'Butcher'.

Charles escaped, in spite of the £30,000 reward for his capture. After roaming round the highlands for nearly six months he was taken to Skye by Flora Macdonald, disguised as her female attendant. From there he escaped to France, later living in Rome and in Florence, looked after by his illegitimate daughter Charlotte, whom he created Duchess of Albany and whom King Louis XVI of France legitimated. It is best to leave Charles at this point, as the romantic, dashing young man, full of courage, enthusiasm and a real sense of mission and who endured so many misfortunes so cheerfully, ended his life a sad and hopeless alcoholic.

He was succeeded in his pretensions by his brother Henry, Duke of York, He was a Cardinal and was generally known as the Cardinal of

York or by local Jacobites as Henry IX. He was a good though strict churchman and was never implicated in any attempts to recover the throne. He lived in Italy and died at Frascati in 1807. The monument to him, his brother and father, partly paid for by the Prince of Wales, later King George IV, is in St Peter's, Rome, a rather pathetic tribute to a sad, proud, romantic line.

But for the Act of Settlement excluding Catholics from the throne, Henry IX would have been succeeded by Charles I's great-great-grand-son, Charles Emmanuel IV of Sardinia. Eventually the Crown would have devolved upon Prince Albert Leopold Ferdinand Michael of Bavaria, present head of the royal house of Bavaria and senior heir general to all the Plantagenets except Henry IV, V and VI, the Tudors and the Stuarts.

Ernest, Duke of Cumberland

'Butcher' Cumberland died without issue in 1765. The next royal duke to bear this title was George III's brother, Henry Frederick, who was so created in 1766. He also had no children, although one Mrs Olivia Serres unsuccessfully claimed to be his legitimate daughter by a secret marriage contracted in 1767, and the title again became extinct in 1790. Nine years later it was bestowed on Prince Ernest Augustus, fifth son of King George III.

Ernest, Duke of Cumberland and Teviotdale, was a most unusual fel-low. His brothers were by and large reasonably intelligent, uninhibited, extroverted, pleasure-loving princes, about whose heads scandals buzzed like flies and with about as much effect. Cumberland was different. He was taciturn, a fierce disciplinarian, a dedicated reactionary Tory and one who kept his private life very much to himself. This secrecy led to the wildest rumours being circulated abroad and the Duke of Cum-berland came to be regarded as some sort of strange bogeyman.

Events, which seem trivial in the retelling, added support to the popu-lar conception of a sinister, evil prince. He was supposed to have murdered Sellis, his valet, in 1810, although the evidence clearly pointed to Sellis having tried to murder the duke and then cut his own throat with a razor.

In 1815 the duke married his cousin, the twice-widowed Princess

Frederica of Mecklenburg-Strelitz, who had jilted the duke's popular brother the Duke of Cambridge and so caused a national scandal. It was also widely rumoured that she had murdered her two previous husbands. Queen Charlotte, the duke's mother, would never receive the new duchess and parliament refused to grant the duke the increase in income usually accorded to a prince of the blood on his marriage. It was ten years before Cumberland received the £6,000 he sought.

It is not surprising that in the circumstances he went to live abroad, only occasionally visiting his brother George, who disliked him but was clearly influenced by his brother's sharp intellect and uncompromising Tory principles. Twelve years later he returned to champion the Protestant–Tory cause in opposing Roman Catholic emancipation which the Tory Duke of Wellington reluctantly supported in parliament, and he remained to stay.

It is hard to understand the almost pathological hatred and fear felt for the duke. Scandal after scandal was spread about him. He was said to have committed incest with his sister Sophia and been the father of one Captain Garth, who was in fact almost certainly the princess's son by General Garth; he was supposed to have assaulted Lady Lyndhurst, wife of the Lord Chancellor and finally he was believed, admittedly only by the *canaille*, to have seduced Lord Graves's wife, a mature lady and mother of fifteen, and so been the cause of his lordship cutting his throat. Cumberland was upset by these calumnies and even brought and won a libel action against one who published the old story of the murder of the valet. But he stayed on in England until, in 1837, on the death of William IV, he succeeded as next male heir to the throne of Hanover.

Although neither kingship nor old age affected Cumberland's extreme Toryism, he ruled Hanover wisely and well for fourteen years. His subjects, although many had liberal tendencies, respected his wisdom and the strength with which he resisted any attempt by Prussia to swallow up his little kingdom. Perhaps his strange character, which was so totally unacceptable to the English, was better understood by the Germans, who he more closely resembled.

The King was devoted to his unpopular wife who, he wrote, 'knew how to tranquillise my mind when irritated and disgusted at all the ingratitude and hostility I met'. Their son George, who succeeded as King of Hanover, became totally blind when he was only fourteen, which must have been a sad cross for the crusty old monarch to bear. Although almost certainly more sinned against than sinning, Ernest, King of Hanover, is one of the more interesting and least typical of all the royal siblings.

As a postscript it should be recounted that the blind king lost his throne when Hanover was annexed to Prussia in 1866. His son Ernest Augustus was deprived of his British titles by Order in Council in 1919 and died in 1923. His grandson, also Ernest Augustus, is the present Prince of Hanover and his young brother George William is married to the Duke of Edinburgh's youngest sister Sophie.

6

ROYAL BASTARDS

Until comparatively recently, the natural child was penalised by both the civil and the common law. On the face of it, this seems hard on such children, but they suffered in what was held to be a good cause, the sanctity of holy matrimony. Marriage has always been held to be the one way of establishing proof of paternity and, if some suffering were caused by the laws relating to bastardy, comfort could be drawn from Lord Chief Justice Coke's words, 'It is better, saith the law, to suffer a mischief to one, than an inconvenience that may prejudice many'. In other words, hard cases make bad law.

Whatever one's views on the rights of bastards may be, it is certain that the illegitimate children of royalty suffered far less than most others, for although, like other bastards they were born without names, honours, or rights of inheritance, they were frequently well provided for by their royal sires.

It is certain that many of our kings have begot illegitimate children but they should not be censured too severely on this account. It is probably true to say that the accepted custom of having one or more concubines was principally due to the fact that royal marriages were generally based on political expediency rather than enduring passion and so were unfulfilling. Whatever the reason, the fact remains that our kings have left many more descendants than are to be found detailed in printed pedigrees of the royal family.

Probably the most prolific monarch in this respect was King Henry I. He left so many illegitimate children that there remains some doubt as to exactly who was and who was not a royal bastard; however, we can positively identify about nine sons and eleven daughters.

In 1120 William, the king's only legitimate son and heir, upon whom the hopes of a peaceful succession to the throne were centred, was returning from a visit to France in a vessel called *The White Ship*. It struck a rock and all save one of the large company on board were drowned. In that company were the king's bastard son Richard, whose body was washed ashore many days after the wreck, and also his daughter Maud, wife of Rotou 'The Great' Count of Perche. It was her screams that were heard by her half brother William and caused them both to be drowned.

Although Henry had many mistresses, Sybil Corbet is usually credited with being the mother of Reynold, Earl of Cornwall, who died on a crusade, William, Sybil, wife of King Alexander I of Scotland who died childless, Gundred and Rohese, who married Henry de la Pomerai.

One of Henry's most noted children was Robert, created Earl of Gloucester in 1122. He and another Robert, also one of Henry's bastards, both supported the claim of their half-sister, the Empress Maud, to succeed to the throne on the death of their father.

Another of Henry's mistresses was Nest, daughter of Rhys ap Tudor, ruler of Deheubarth, an old Welsh kingdom in the south west. By this noble lady he had a son Henry. The king was also known to be the father of three other sons, Gilbert, William de Tracy and Fulk, who probably became a monk.

His bastard daughters mostly made good marriages. Maud married Conan III, Duke of Brittany, Constance (or she may have been called Maud) married Roscelin de Beaumont, and Alice, or Aline, married Matthew de Montmorenci, Constable of France. Juliane married Eustace de Pacy and by him had two daughters. These were at one time given to Ralph Harenc as hostages in exchange for his son. Eustace was cruel and unwise enough to blind the young hostage, whereupon the king allowed Harenc to have his revenge by blinding the two girls and also cutting off the tips of their noses. A daughter, Isabel, apparently died unmarried and another Maud, who was probably the king's child, became Abbess of Montivilliers.

The life and death of Henry II's mistress 'Fair Rosamond', the daughter of Walter de Clifford, is a maze of legends and suppositions. One thing seems certain, she was buried in the church at Godstow nunnery, just outside Oxford. Whether she was hidden from the jealousy of Henry's wife Eleanor in the royal palace of Woodstock hard by Godstow, and there discovered by the queen and either bled to death in a hot bath, or poisoned, is something we shall probably never know.

Two sons by Henry are attributed to her, William Longespée, or Longsword, Earl of Salisbury, a faithful royal servant, and Geoffrey, who became Archbishop of York, but never saw eye to eye with the Chapter of the Cathedral and eventually fled abroad. He died in 1212 and is buried at Grandmont, near Rouen. In fact, it seems certain that although Geoffrey and William were Henry's sons, it would have been chronologically impossible for Rosamond to have been their mother.

King Richard I, 'Coeur de Lion', is known to have had a bastard son Philip, who died in about 1211. His brother, King John, was the father of a daughter Joan, who married Llywelyn the Great, ruler of all Wales, and from whom the Queen is directly descended.

King Edward I had nineteen legitimate children by his two wives, but he also had a bastard son, John de Bottetourt, who was summoned to parliament as baron and served in his father's expeditions to Gascony and Scotland. He died in 1324.

Although John of Gaunt, son of Edward III, was never king, mention must be made of his bastard children by Katherine Swynford, daughter of Sir Payne Roet. These were the famous Beauforts: John, Henry, Thomas and Joan. All were born before their father married Katherine. In 1397 their cousin, King Richard II, by Letters Patent read in parliament, thus giving them the full force of a statute, legitimated all four of them. The patent stated that 'of our special prerogative, favour and grace ... yielding to the prayers of our said uncle your begetter and to you who, as it is said, suffer from a defect of birth ... we will that notwithstanding this ... you be able to be preferred, promoted, chosen, placed and admitted to any kind of honours, dignities, pre-eminences, estates, ranks and offices, public and private, as well perpetual as temporal, both feudal and noble, by whatsoever name they be called, even if they be dukedoms, principalities ... or other fiefs ... and that you may receive, hold, bear and exercise them freely and lawfully as if you were born of a lawful union ... and by the assent of parliament by the tenor of these presents we dispense and restore you and each of you in birth and legitimate you.'

I have quoted this patent rather extensively because after the words '... placed and admitted to any kind of honours, dignities ...' there has been interpolated the phrase 'except royal dignity'. In other words the legitimation was good for all purposes save succession to the throne. Yet, it seems clear that the interpolation was almost certainly made after the sealing and reading of the patent and is, therefore, a forgery. In 1407, a further patent was issued by Henry IV which merely exemplifies the words of the earlier patent, but includes in the actual original, engrossed text the interpolated words. This later document, if the phrase referring to the royal dignity is indeed a forgery, has no effect, being but a restatement of Richard II's intentions, which has led all historians to declare unequivocally that the Beauforts were legally debarred from the succession.

The Beauforts symbolised their legitimation by discarding the bastardized versions of their coats of arms in favour of the royal arms, differenced from those of the king by the addition of borders round the arms. Upon being legitimated, John, the eldest son, born at Beaufort Castle, Anjou (hence the reason for the surname) in about 1373, was created Earl of Somerset and a few months later Marquess of Dorset and Somerset. Henry, the second son, became Bishop of Winchester and, in 1426, was created a cardinal. Thomas, the youngest son, was created Earl of Dorset and in 1416 Duke of Exeter for life, but he died without surviving issue ten years later. Joan, the only daughter, married firstly Robert Ferrers, Lord Ferrers of Wemme and, after his death, Ralph Nevill, Earl of Westmorland. By her two husbands, she had no less than fifteen children.

The Marquess of Somerset's second son, John, was created Duke of Somerset in 1443, his only child Margaret being the mother of King Henry VII. His next son Edmund was created Duke of Somerset after his brother's death. His eldest son, Henry, second duke of the second creation, had a bastard son Charles Somerset, who was created Earl of Worcester in 1514. In 1682 his descendant Henry, sixth Earl and third Marquess of Worcester was created Duke of Beaufort and from him is descended the present Duke, who is Master of the Horse and, more important still, at least in the eyes of the hunting fraternity, master of the famous Beaufort hunt.

King Edward IV had a bastard son named Arthur Plantagenet, possibly the son of either Elizabeth Lucy, Jane Shore or Elizabeth Waite. He married the daughter of Edward Grey, Viscount Lisle, a title which was later conferred on him. He was suspected of being implicated in a plot and was imprisoned in the Tower. It is said that the poor man died of excitement on hearing that the king had declared him innocent and ordered his release.

Henry Fitzroy, Duke of Richmond and Somerset, was Henry VIII's son by Elizabeth Blount. He was born in 1519. When it became clear that Queen Catherine of Aragon was not going to produce a son for Henry, his seven year old bastard was created a duke, given precedence over all peers and even over his half-sister, Princess Mary. A princely household was assigned to him and he was made Lord High Admiral, Lord Warden of the Marches and Lord Lieutenant of Ireland. No one could be oblivious of the significance of these moves. If Henry was not to sire a legitimate son, he clearly had it in mind to make his bastard the heir-apparent. It was probably providential that he died in 1536, just before Queen Jane Seymour gave birth to a son for, with the succession secured, he would have been an embarrassment to his royal father.

When people think of royal bastards, they at once think of that 'Merry Monarch', Charles II, whose illegitimate progeny was quite a feature, almost a symbol, of life after the Restoration.

Of his various mistresses, Barbara Villiers bore him the most children and had the greatest influence over him. She was the daughter of William, Viscount Grandison, the wife of Lord Castlemaine, and Charles created her Duchess of Cleveland, Countess of Southampton and Baroness Nonsuch. She was said to be a woman of great beauty, but 'most enormously viscious and revenous; foolish but imperious; very uneasy to the King, and always carrying on intrigues with other men.' There is some doubt as to whether her daughter Anne, wife of the Earl of Sussex, was Charles' or her husband's child, but her sons Charles Fitzroy, Duke of Southampton and Cleveland, Henry Fitzroy, Duke of Grafton, and George Fitzroy, Duke of Northumberland, were acknowledged by Charles as his sons. He referred to them as his 'dear and natural sons' when he granted them bastardised versions of his royal arms and, as has been seen, also ennobled all of them. Of the three titles only the dukedom of Grafton still exists, the present and eleventh duke being in the forefront of the movement to preserve ancient buildings, whilst his wife is Mistress of the Robes to the Queen.

The Duchess of Cleveland also had a daughter, Charlotte, who married the Earl of Lichfield. The duchess may have influenced the king and been 'very uneasy' to him, but she is not the best known of Charles's courtesans. In this respect the accolade must undoubtedly be bestowed on Nell Gwyn. She was not highly born, she acquired no titles and she left politics to others, but there is something appealing about the young, beautiful girl, brought up in a brothel, who graduated to selling oysters, then oranges and lastly taking to the boards and being picked up by a king when only seventeen. He was her third Charles. Her first was Charles Hart, a great-nephew of William Shakespeare and manager of the King's Theatre, where Nell acted. Her second Charles was Lord Buckhurst, and the king was the third Charles to seduce her. She bore him two sons, Charles and James Beauclerk. The latter died in 1680, but the former was created Duke of St Albans and is the ancestor of the present duke. She died two years after her paramour.

If Nelly, 'The Protestant Whore', is the best known and in her day the most popular of Charles's mistresses, James Scott (also known as Crofts and Fitz Roy), Duke of Monmouth, son of Lucy Walters, is the best known of Charles's bastards, as well as being his first acknowledged and favourite son. He was born at The Hague in 1649 and was cared for by Lord Crofts. Charles created him Duke of Monmouth in 1663, in which year he married Anne Scott, whose name he took, Countess of Buccleuch. Monmouth was a champion of Protestantism and many who saw danger in the Catholic James succeeding his brother Charles, looked to Monmouth as a future king. It was rumoured that his parents had been secretly married and that the evidence of the marriage was to be found in a 'black box'.

It is to Charles' credit that, although he admired and loved his son, he would never acknowledge him as legitimate and so heir-apparent. 'I will not yield, nor will I be bullied' he said, 'I have law and reason and all right-thinking men on my side.' This was a brave stand for legitimate succession as it would have been so easy to court popularity and keep close to the son he loved above all his other children. As it was, father and son were estranged. Monmouth was not at Charles's bedside when he died, having himself embraced Roman Catholicism, but was plotting to overthrow his half-uncle James and seize the crown. His rebellion failed and he died on the scaffold, stripped of his honours. Monmouth and his wife had been created Duke and Duchess of Buccleuch on their marriage, so that his wife's dukedom, not being forfeited, passed to their eldest grandson on her death in 1732. Thus, the ninth and present Duke of Buccleuch, nephew of Princess Alice, Duchess of Gloucester, is a direct descendant of the luckless Duke of Monmouth.

By Catherine Pegge, later Lady Green, Charles had two children, Charles FitzCharles, Earl of Plymouth, and Catherine who probably became a Benedictine nun at Dunkirk and who died, a very old lady indeed, in 1759.

Mary Davies, a singer and actress, was the mother of a daughter by Charles, Lady Mary Tudor. William Pepys relates that 'it seems she is a bastard of Colonel Howard, my Lord Berkshire, and that he hath got her for the king'. She was certainly a popular dancer, the 'delight of all the nobler sort, pride of the stage, and darling of the Court'. Her daughter married successively Edward Radclyffe, Earl of Derwentwater, Henry Graham and James Rooke.

Most of Charles's bastards had but one Christian name. The exception was Charlotte Jemima Henrietta Maria, whose mother was Elizabeth, daughter of Sir Robert Killigrew and wife of Francis Boyle, Viscount Shannon. She was born in 1650 and it may be that her last two names were chosen because they were those of Charles II's mother, to whom Sir Robert Killigrew was at one time vice-chamberlain. Charlotte was twice married, firstly to James Howard and then to William Paston, Earl of Yarmouth.

Charles was devoted to his youngest sister 'Minette' (Henrietta, Duchess of Orleans). When Minette was in England in 1670, cementing the Anglo-French alliance, she brought with her a charming, aristocratic girl called Louise de Keroualle. A few weeks later Minette died and King Louis XIV of France, to console Charles and make certain of maintaining his influence at the English Court, sent him Louise as a maid-of-honour to the Queen. She was quickly established as the chief royal mistress, was naturalised and created Duchess of Portsmouth for life. Charles also procured for her from King Louis the fief of Aubigny in France. Her only child by Charles was Charles Lennox, who was created Duke of Richmond in England and of Lennox in Scotland. He died before his mother, but his son inherited the French dukedom of Aubigny on the death of Louise in 1734. The ninth and present duke is the owner of the famous Goodwood racecourse.

James II, like his brother Charles, had an illegitimate family but this fact is not so well known as his sons flourished on the continent rather than in Britain. By his mistress Arabella Churchill, sister of the great Duke of Marlborough, he had two sons and two daughters.

Although the Count de Grammont called poor Arabella 'a tall creature, pale-faced, nothing but skin and bone', her eldest son James Fitzjames was accounted handsome and, when his father came to the throne, was created Duke of Berwick. He was a noted soldier, eventually becoming a Marshal of France and it is curious to recollect that whilst his uncle, the Duke of Marlborough, was fighting against the King of France he was fighting for that same king in Spain. In 1734, when in command of the French army of the Rhine, his head was blown off by a cannonball at the battle of Philipsbourg. His eldest son's line are to be found in Spain as Dukes of Alba, Liria and Berwick, whilst his eldest son by his second marriage became Duke of Fitzjames in France.

Berwick's younger brother, Henry, was created titular Duke of Albemarle by his father in exile, but he lived in France and left no descendants. One of Arabella's daughters became a nun, whilst the other, Henrietta, married Sir Henry Waldegrave, later Lord Waldegrave and ancestor of the present earl.

King George I's reign may be truly said to have got off to a bad start from which it never recovered. The king was a shy man with narrow vision and was unable to speak English. His young wife had committed adultery with Count Königsmark in 1694 and George had had her imprisoned in the Castle of Ahlden, where she remained until her death thirty-two years later. This treatment of his wife did not endear him to his new subjects any more than his importation of two unattractive

German mistresses, known as 'The Maypole' and 'The Elephant and Castle'; for one, Ehrengard Melusina, Baroness von der Schulenberg, was thin and skinny and the other, Charlotte Sophia, Baroness von Kielmansegge, was gross. To add insult to injury, the Schulenberg was created Duchess of Kendal and the Kielmansegge, Countess of Darlington.

The Duchess of Kendal bore the king two daughters, Petronille—who was created Countess of Walsingham in 1722 and married Philip Stanhope, Earl of Chesterfield—and Margaret, who married the Count of Lippe. Lady Darlington was the mother of Mary, Viscountess Howe, but her husband rather than her lover was probably the father, although the king paid the Viscountess a pension on the Irish Exchequer.

King George II is said to have remarked to his wife, 'you must love the Wallmoden, for she loves me'. The Wallmoden was the beautiful Amelie Sophie, wife of Adam, Count von Wallmoden and a niece of the Duchess of Kendal. She became George's mistress and was created Countess of Yarmouth. George is sometimes said to have fathered her youngest child, Johann von Wallmoden who was brought up at Court, and became a field-marshal in the Hanoverian army, but he never acknowledged paternity.

George's great-grandson, King George IV is notorious for his amours and the general laxity of his morals, but he never publicly acknowledged any bastards. It is probably for this reason that nearly all those who have illusions of grandeur, believing they must have royal blood in their veins, adopt lusty George as their ancestor. No one can prove whether they are right or wrong, but of all those who claim descent from the natural children of George, most must, at the best, be guilty of wishful thinking.

The last king publicly to acknowledge his bastards was King William IV. In 1791, when Duke of Clarence, he set up house with a well known actress, Mrs Dorothy Jordan, 'Little Pickle'. She was older than her royal lover and had already had various illegitimate children by other paramours, but she and the Duke of Clarence managed to lead what can only be called a happy, middle-class, unmarried life.

They had a family of nine children, four sons and five daughters. Dorothy died in 1816 and was buried at St Cloud, but when William came to the throne some years later he created his eldest son, George FitzClarence, Earl of Munster, Viscount FitzClarence and Baron

Tewkesbury. To those of his other children who had not obtained higher precedence by marriage, he granted the title and precedence of the younger issue of a marquess. The present Earl of Munster has held various offices in Conservative governments since before the second world war, being Minister without Portfolio from 1954 to 1957.

7

ROYAL RESIDENCES

Although most people think of Buckingham Palace as the principal, formal residence and seat of the Queen and her Court, there are two other palaces which are perhaps even more closely connected with the official business of the Crown. They are St James's Palace and the Palace of Westminster.

Westminster

The Palace of Westminster is better known as the Houses of Parliament, because it is the seat of government, but it is also a royal palace. When the Queen issues Letters Patent under the Great Seal, these begin with the salutation, 'Elizabeth the Second by the Grace of God of the United Kingdom of Great Britain and Northern Ireland and of Our other Realms and Territories Queen Head of the Commonwealth Defender of the Faith. To all to whom these Presents shall come Greeting.' And they close with the words 'Witness Ourself at Westminster' followed by the date. In fact, the Queen signs the warrants wherever she may be at the time, but officially this is always at Westminster.

The present Palace of Westminster was built after the old palace—save only Westminster Hall and the crypt of St Stephen's Chapel—was destroyed by fire in 1835, but the first palace dates from before the Norman conquest.

Canute may have built a palace on the site, but Edward the Confessor certainly did, together with a church and a monastery. William II built the great hall, which is almost 240 feet long, and which was later rebuilt with a hammer-beam roof by Richard II. At Whitsun in 1099 he held court at Westminster and, thereafter, it came to be used more and more as the legal centre of the kingdom. St Stephen's Chapel was built by King Stephen, and the famous crypt, much favoured by Members of Parliament for the baptism of their infants, by King Edward I. Thomas Becket restored the palace after it had been despoiled by Stephen's followers, but it was Henry III who put Westminster firmly on the map as the hub and centre of government and justice; he also spent almost £30,000 on the fabric and on the nearby abbey.

Many succeeding monarchs made their mark on Westminster. King John added a lavatory, Richard II a bath with hot and cold running water and King Edward III a prison, known as the 'House called Hell'. Fire destroyed much of the palace in 1512 after which it was not again used as a royal residence, although it remained the seat of government.

The hall, now noted as the place where sovereigns and great men lie in state, has been the scene of many famous state trials and also of the great banquets which, until the coronation of King William IV, followed upon the crowning ceremony.

As I have mentioned, most of the palace was destroyed in 1834 and a competition was held for designing a new building, which had to be either Gothic or Elizabethan in style. Charles Barry won the competition and in 1840 the first stone of the present building, not officially opened until 1852, was laid. There is no doubt that Barry's Gothic design was magnificent and ideally suited for the permanence, grandeur and majesty which should attend the government of a great empire. At least, there is no doubt in my mind. The proportions, the wood and stone carving, the paintings and stained glass are exquisite and a tribute not only to the best of Victorian Gothic architecture, but to the genius of Sir Charles Barry and his friend, Augustus Welby Pugin, head of the wood-carving department and Barry's able lieutenant. It was fitting that the flag on the Victoria Tower was flown at half-mast on 22nd May 1860, on which day Barry was laid to rest in Edward the Confessor's Abbey of St Peter at Westminster.

St James's Palace

In that dull but informative section of the more literate daily newspapers, called 'The Court Circular', notices frequently appear to the effect that

Mr So and So presented his credentials as Ambassador Extraordinary and Minister Plenipotentiary for such and such a country at the Court of St James. Does the Queen then drive down to St James's Palace to receive new ambassadors at her Court there? No: no more than she signs documents at Westminster. It is a legacy from a past age; a fiction which no one has thought to alter.

In Norman times, St James's Palace was a hospital for leprous females, being dedicated to St James the Less, Bishop of Jerusalem. Henry VI made it over to his college at Eton, but Henry VIII gave the fellows of Eton some lands in Suffolk in exchange for the old hospital. He pensioned off the patients and built a hunting lodge and palace on the site. On the old gateway, facing the end of St James's Street, can still be seen Henry's initial entwined with an 'A', commemorating the fact that the palace was once a home for Anne Boleyn.

This comfortable, homely Tudor palace, constructed in red and blue brick and composed of four courts, was used as a residence by Queen Mary I who died there, and by Henry, Prince of Wales, eldest son of James I. He lived there in some state, having a retinue of over four hundred persons and it was he who started to amass a fine collection of *objects d'art*, which was continued after his death by Queen Henrietta Maria. She lived there with her Catholic Court but, like many another royal palace, it was taken over by the Roundheads, who sold the treasures and used the palace as a military prison and barracks.

After Restoration, some of Charles II's mistresses lived in St James's and James II's son, the Old Pretender, was born there; or, for those who prefer romance to fact, a child given out as being the Queen's was smuggled into her room in a warming pan to provide a Catholic heir to the throne.

When Whitehall was burned down in 1698 the Court moved to St James's and it remained the official residence of the sovereign and his Court until King George III bought Buckingham Palace. Thereafter, it continued to be used for occasional levées and drawing-rooms, to house junior members of the royal family and it is also used sometimes for official receptions. The accession and coronation of a sovereign are still proclaimed by the heralds at St James's, which serves as a reminder that the official Court of St James remains, although the actual Court moved away ages since.

Some of the palace was destroyed by fire in 1809, but much remains and houses that most important department of the royal household, the Office of the Lord Chamberlain.

Buckingham Palace

Buckingham House was built by a Dutch architect, Captain Wynde, for John Sheffield, Duke of Buckingham and Normanby. King George III, who easily wearied of the stiff manners of the Hanoverian Court at St James's, bought it from the duke's bastard son as a domestic retreat in 1762, and all his many children were born there.

George III built new wings and John Nash was employed by George IV to alter the whole building at a cost of almost £75,000. It was he who designed the Marble Arch surmounted by a statue of the monarch on horseback, which stood where the east wing (the main range seen by the public and which looks down the Mall) now is. This wing, designed by Edward Blore, was added by Queen Victoria and the arch was resited at the north east corner of Hyde Park, where Tyburn gallows used to stand.

A south wing, designed by Sir James Pennethorne, was also added by Victoria and George V had the whole of Blore's east front, originally built in soft Caen stone, refaced with Portland stone.

Although Victoria left the palace after her husband's death in 1861, subsequent monarchs have made it the principal home and seat of the Court.

Whitehall

Mention has been made of Whitehall, the seat of the Court until it moved to St James's Palace. From 1248 until the fall of Cardinal Wolsey in 1531, Whitehall, then known as York Place, was the London palace of the Archbishops of York. With Wolsey out of the way, King Henry VIII took the palace, enlarged it and spent much time there. Where Horseguards' Parade stands today there was a tilt yard, an inevitable attachment to any house inhabited by Henry, and all around was a veritable warren of buildings, straggling over many acres. It was among this populous, rambling Court, conveniently close to Whitehall, that Henry breathed his last.

His younger daughter, Queen Elizabeth I, built what we might call a 'pre-fab' banqueting hall made of wood and canvas and containing 292 panes of glass. It took a month to erect. James I decided to build a permanent hall, which he did in 1606, but it was claimed only thirteen years later by that remorseless enemy of royal and other buildings, fire. Undeterred, he rebuilt the hall, this time in Portland stone. This hall, which is a perfect double cube, being 110 feet long and 55 broad, still stands in Whitehall and is open to the public. James envisaged his hall as part of a vast new palace, but for fiscal reasons this dream never got further than Inigo Jones's drawing board. Had it been built, it would have been one of the finest buildings of its time, being composed of seven courts, one encompassing an inner, circular 'Persian court'.

It was on a scaffold built outside one of the windows of James's hall that his son Charles went, by way of the headman's axe 'from corruptible to incorruptible crown, where no disturbance can be'.

After the restoration of Charles II, Whitehall came into its own. Here Charles essayed to imitate the fabulous splendour of the Court of King Louis XIV of France, the 'Sun King'. Here his mistresses were smuggled in and out of his chamber by his faithful servant William Chiffinch; here he played tennis, gamed, wined and dined amidst a mass of courtiers, dogs, caged birds and foreign ambassadors; and here eventually the 'Merry Monarch' died, just thirteen years before fire destroyed all but James's magnificent banqueting hall.

The Tower of London

It is sometimes forgotten that the Tower of London is not just an ancient prison haunted by innumerable headless spectres, shades of those who entered the Tower from the river by Traitor's Gate and left it by way of the block; nor is it simply a strong room containing the crown jewels, carefully guarded by 'Beefeaters' and ravens: it is also a royal palace.

Having said that, it is only fair to state that it was never built as a luxury dwelling. When William the Conqueror built the White Tower in 1078 he saw to it that the walls were 15 feet thick at the base and arrow slits served as windows until Sir Christopher Wren put in glazed casements six hundred years later. There were also some uncomfortable dungeons and a sword room, not usual features of a gentleman's town house. No, the Tower was a fortress built to protect London from invasion by water and to be a grim and permanent symbol of royal power and justice.

A wall with thirteen towers which environed the Tower was destroyed by Oliver Cromwell, fire and decay, having been built by King Henry III, who also started a menagerie in the Tower. This remained a feature of the place until it was removed to the London Zoo in the early nineteenth century.

Edward I added an outer wall, so that there was then a keep with an inner and outer bailey.

Although succeeding kings used the Tower formally, almost symbolically, as a palace, in that it was from there that they left for their coronations, it was more and more employed as a prison and a place of execution. In Tudor times, it was also a mint, armoury and treasury but never the home of the sovereign.

Today the Tower, though a number one tourist attraction, is still a royal liberty and is governed by a constable appointed by the Crown and, of course, it still houses the precious symbols of sovereignty.

Windsor Castle

Another royal residence which was built as a fortress but which, unlike the Tower, was also used and still is used as a country palace, is Windsor Castle.

Like the Tower it was erected by William I to guard that main artery of England, the river Thames. It was not an impregnable keep, as was the Tower, but a motte and bailey castle built of wood. Henry II rebuilt it in stone with the round tower on its commanding mound, which is still a feature of the castle.

King Henry III was the first king to make the castle more like a home and he also built a defensive wall around it. It was at Windsor that King Edward III, who spent much money on the castle, instituted the Order of the Garter and he made Windsor the home of his new Order. There it had its chapel, dedicated, like the Order, to St George, and there provision was made for poor knights to live and fulfil vicariously the

Windsor Castle

religious obligations of the members of the Order. The Military Knights of Windsor, as they are now called, still live within the castle walls and say the knights' prayers for them in St George's Chapel.

The present chapel is not the one which King Richard II restored with the help of his clerk of the works, Geoffrey Chaucer, but is that built in its place by King Edward IV.

The castle itself was much improved by Queen Elizabeth I, who added the long gallery, which is now the library. However, she did not often resort to Windsor as she found it damp and cold. James I probably felt the same about it, but he enjoyed the hunting there and so was often at the castle in the pursuit of his favourite sport.

In the civil war, Prince Rupert's royalist forces attacked the castle after the battle of Edgehill, but with little effect. It remained in the hands of the Roundheads and was used as a prison during the Commonwealth. Charles II put it in order and had the famous long walk made.

Queen Anne went to Windsor for the hunting, but preferred to stay at a house she bought just outside the castle, later known as Queen's Lodge. The Hanoverians eschewed Windsor and when George III eventually went there, typically, he preferred the homely atmosphere and vastly superior plumbing of Queen's Lodge to the slowly decaying, cold grandeur of the castle. Nevertheless, he was prudent enough to have the main castle restored by James Wyatt in the Gothic manner. Thereafter, George made history by being the first king to die at Windsor, being buried in St George's Chapel.

James Wyatt's nephew, Jeffry, who affected the name of Wyattville, was employed by George IV to continue his uncle's work and make the whole concept more romantic, with grand state apartments. The result is the Windsor Castle of today, still a retreat of the royal family who like to ride in the great park, or that part of it not now a safari park, and they use it as a base in the polo season and when Ascot races are being run.

The great tragedy of Windsor today is that it not only commands the middle reaches of the Thames, but also the flight path from London Airport. A peaceful picnic in the shadow of the castle walls can be a shattering experience.

Holyrood House

All the palaces and castles noted so far have been in England. What of the royal residences in Scotland? Where does the Queen stay and hold Court when she goes, as she frequently does, north of the border?

The official Scottish royal palace is Holyrood House in Edinburgh. It was originally founded in 1128 by King David I, as an abbey for the canons regular of St Augustine. It is for this reason that the street which leads from Edinburgh Castle down to the abbey is called Canongate.

At first the Scottish kings lived in the castle, but they eventually moved into the guest house of the abbey, which King James IV developed into a palace for his bride, Margaret, daughter of King Henry VII of England. His son, James V, added a south wing and although part of the building was destroyed when it was attacked by the Duke of Somerset on the orders of King Henry VIII, Mary Queen of Scots lived there and Holyrood House was the scene of her famous debates on religion with John Knox and also of the murder of her unpopular favourite, David Riccio.

In the civil war, Holyrood became a barracks and suffered some depredation, but Charles II employed Sir William Bruce of Kinross to rebuild it. This he did by adding a tower to balance that built by James IV and then linking the two towers with a building in the Palladian manner, albeit somewhat restrained owing to shortage of funds.

He also commissioned a Dutch painter named de Witte to paint a hundred portraits of the Scottish kings at £2 a picture, to help furnish the palace.

Charles II never managed to see his handywork and, apart from a brief but historic visit made by the Young Pretender before his ill-fated attempt to seize the crown in 1745, the palace remained unvisited until George IV held a levée there. This levée, arranged by Sir Walter Scott, was typically theatrical, the monarch appearing in flesh-coloured tights and kilt. It was not repeated, but thereafter the royal family has made occasional visits to the palace and once a year it becomes the official residence of the Lord High Commissioner, who is the Queen's representative at the meeting of the General Assembly of the Church of Scotland.

Balmoral

The Queen's home in Scotland is not the Palace of Holyrood House, but Balmoral. Queen Victoria first discovered Balmoral in Aberdeenshire and obtained a lease of it in 1848. It was a very small house and she and Prince Albert used to retreat there and lead an entirely rustic and informal life 'like private gentlefolks, but like very small gentlefolks'.

Then, quite out of the blue, one J. C. Nield left the Queen a sizeable fortune. Victoria, surprised but delighted, spent £31,500 of this fairy money on buying Balmoral and the surrounding estate of 17,400 acres.

She had the little house pulled down and spent some of the remaining money on commissioning William Smith of Aberdeen to erect a much larger building in the towered and turreted style, generally known as Scottish baronial. Balmoral has remained the favourite Scottish retreat of the royal family, who holiday there most summers.

Sandringham

The English equivalent to Balmoral is Sandringham, near King's Lynn in Norfolk. It is an Elizabethan-style house which, with the accompanying estate, was bought by King Edward VII mainly for the shooting. When he died, his widow, Queen Alexandra, lived and eventually died

Balmoral Castle

The Sheel of Allt na Giuthasach, on the Balmoral estate.

there. It was always a favourite haunt of King George V and he and Queen Mary moved in and ran it as an English country residence and estate should be run. Sandringham is still a model estate and it is a lucky person who is a tenant there.

Kensington Palace

William III bought Nottingham House from Heneage Finch, Earl of Nottingham, for 18,000 guineas. Almost at once part of it was burnt down and he employed Sir Christopher Wren to rebuild it. The result was what is today called Kensington Palace, the home of Princess Margaret, and Princess Alice, Countess of Athlone; it is also where the London offices of various minor members of the royal family are housed.

Both Mary II and William III died in their new London home, the former of small-pox, the latter of pneumonia.

Queen Anne liked Kensington, as she was fond of gardens and the palace had twenty-six acres of garden. She made some alterations to the formal gardens and built the orangery, designed by either Vanburgh or Hawksmoor, which is still a noted feature of the house. Like her sister and brother-in-law, she died at Kensington.

Kensington also caught the fancy of King George I, who did much to improve it. He had the gardens landscaped and the Round Pond made, while in the house William Kent added new state apartments, including the cupola room, where Queen Victoria was baptised. He also added the king's staircase, which is painted with a vast *trompe-d'oeil* of balconies crowded with courtiers and Yeomen of the Guard.

Queen Victoria's parents had apartments at Kensington and she was brought up there. Queen Mary also once lived there and always preferred its more intimate atmosphere to the grandeur of Buckingham Palace.

In 1899 the palace was restored and, except for the residential apartments, may be visited by the public.

Hampton Court

Hampton Court was once a great royal palace and still belongs to the Crown, although since Queen Victoria's time, it has been open to the public. It was abandoned by King George III and part of the palace has thereafter been used for grace and favour apartments.

Hampton Court originally formed part of the vast estates owned by the Order of St John of Jerusalem, now better known as the Order of Malta. Cardinal Wolsey leased it from the Order for a rent of £50 a year and built a palace there. In 1529, Wolsey gave his palace to King Henry VIII who, after Wolsey's disgrace and death, added greatly to the building. Not only did he endow it with a tilt yard, tennis court and other sporting facilities, but also built a great hall and gallery. The former was much used by Queen Elizabeth I for revels and entertainments at Christmas; indeed, the palace was a popular resort of both Tudor and Stuart monarchs.

During the Commonwealth, Lord Protector Cromwell made it his country house, an unfortunate choice as it transpired, because it was at Hampton Court that Cromwell caught the ague from which he died.

The palace was frequently visited by King William and Queen Mary, who modernised it. Sir Christopher Wren rebuilt about half of the existing house, giving it the symmetrical, classical appearance which characterises the grand front along the canal. Because his work was never finished, the Tudor front, with a gateway approached through a formidable escort of stone beasts, and the courtyard remained unscathed.

Greenwich

Apart from those royal palaces and residences which are still used, or which are an integral part of the continuing history of the country, there are many others which were used for a time and then abandoned for one reason or another. It is not possible to detail all of these, but some of the more famous must be noted.

At Greenwich, there still stands a fair and splendid edifice which, for over a century, has housed the Royal Naval College. This is perhaps why it is sometimes forgotten that Greenwich was once a popular Thames-side palace. Humphrey, Duke of Gloucester, uncle of King Henry VI, acquired Greenwich and built there his 'Manor of Pleasaunce', later called Plesshy. When he died, or was murdered, his manor reverted to the crown and was a favourite resort of Henry VI's wife, Queen Margaret, who improved the building, as did Edward IV, Henry VII and

Henry VIII. The last named and also his daughter Elizabeth were born there. Greenwich was the scene of Sir Walter Raleigh's historic gallantry, when he spread his cloak over the marshy ground to protect the feet of his sovereign, Elizabeth I.

James I gave Greenwich to his queen, Anne of Denmark. She commissioned Inigo Jones to build a little palace behind the riverside palace, where the old gate-house stood. This classical building of exquisite proportions contrasted greatly with the rambling old palace with its three courtyards and irregular battlemented towers. It was called the Queen's House and, after the civil war, Charles II started rebuilding the old palace, which was then much decayed. He never finished this and it was left to Wren to complete what became a hospital for disabled sailors and, in 1869, the present Naval College. The Queen's House was restored after the last war and is now the home of part of the National Maritime Museum.

Richmond

Also on the river, but above London, was the royal palace of Sheen, scene of the death of King Edward III in 1377. Richard II added to the palace by building an annexe to it on an island in the Thames opposite the main palace. However, Queen Anne of Bohemia died at Sheen and Richard, overcome by sorrow, had the palace 'thrown down' and destroyed. Henry V rebuilt it but fire razed it to the ground in the reign of Henry VII. Undaunted, the first Tudor monarch erected yet another palace on the site, a fantasy of domes, pinnacles and turrets which he named Richmond, after his former title of Earl of Richmond.

Elizabeth I died at Richmond, but not before her godson, the wit Sir John Harington, had installed there the first royal flush-lavatory. In the civil war, Richmond was sold to raise money for the parliamentary army and after the restoration it was more or less abandoned. It decayed and was pulled down bit by bit until all that remained was a gateway, which still stands. It is a symbol of the end of the Tudor era, for within the shadow of this gate Sir John Carey waited for news that Queen Elizabeth had breathed her last, the sign for him to ride post haste to summon her cousin, King James VI of Scotland, to come south with all speed to claim the throne.

[176]

Nonsuch

If Richmond was an architectural folly, it was nothing to the prestige palace which Henry VIII built near Cheam in Surrey. In 1538 over five hundred workmen started to build a vast, ornate, gilded half-timbered palace, bedight with domes and cupolas, oriels, battlements and pinnacles. A veritable wedding cake of a palace whose only real purpose was to impress King Francis I of France, reminding him that anything he could do, Henry could do better. It was a sequel to that historic piece of one-upmanship, the Field of the Cloth of Gold. In fact, Henry never even stayed there and Queen Mary I did not want to. She gave it to Henry Fitzalan, Earl of Arundel, in exchange for estates elsewhere.

The earl had ambitions to be Queen Elizabeth I's consort and invited her to Nonsuch, for thus the palace was aptly named. She came and apparently enjoyed herself, if not the company of her ambitious and comparatively elderly host, from whose son-in-law, Lord Lumley, she eventually acquired Nonsuch.

The Queens of James I and Charles I used Nonsuch; the Parliamentary Commissioners sold it and, after the restoration of Charles II, the Treasury moved there for a while to be away from plague-ridden London. Charles II gave it to his mistress, Barbara Villiers, Lady Castlemaine, whom he created, among other things, Baroness Nonsuch, but she did not like the place and eventually sold it for demolition.

Brighton Pavilion

Another royal fantasy, but one which has survived, is the folly known as Brighton Pavilion. This was built in 1787 for George IV and his unlawful wife, Mrs Maria Fitzherbert, by Henry Holland. It is Persian, Chinese and Indian, classical and Palladian and really has to be seen to be appreciated. Nothing remotely like it existed and it is still a place at which to gaze and wonder. The oriental part was added by Nash, whose dragons, lotus flowers and candelabra now characterise the whole building. William Hazlitt said that the Pavilion was like 'a collection of stone pumpkins and pepper boxes. It seems as if the genius of architecture had at once the dropsy and the megrims'.

Certainly it did not amuse Queen Victoria, who sold it to Brighton corporation in 1849.

Osborne

Osborne

Queen Victoria, seeking a little privacy after her marriage to Prince Albert, acquired a property in the Isle of Wight for £26,000 in 1845. The existing house was at once pulled down and Thomas Cubitt built Osborne House, which was partly designed by Prince Albert. Its flat roof and flat-topped towers make it look a little like a grand crematorium, but it is typical of its period. After the death of Albert, it became the Queen's favourite residence and it was there that she died.

King Edward VII gave Osborne to the nation, to be a rest and convalescent home for ex-officers and it still fulfils this useful function.

Woodstock

The last royal palace I am going to mention is one which has long ceased to exist, but which was once a favourite hunting lodge and palace, namely Woodstock in Oxfordshire.

Henry I built it within an enclosed park and it was used more or less frequently by successive monarchs both as a hunting lodge and, in the reign of Henry II for holding councils.

It is famous as the place where Rosamund Clifford, 'Fair Rosamund', the mistress of Henry II, hid from the supposed jealousy of his queen, who later, so it is said—but I suspect without much foundation—discovered and murdered her. Edward the 'Black Prince' was born at Woodstock and was known to his contemporaries as Edward of Woodstock.

When Mary came to the throne she kept her half-sister Elizabeth at Woodstock, under what we would now call 'house arrest'. Her custodian—goaler is too strong a word—was Sir Henry Bedingfeld, who complained of the damp, cold and poor security.

The decrepit palace was eventually ceded by Queen Anne to John Churchill, Duke of Marlborough, the victor of Blenheim. Here Sir John Vanburgh built him a vast palace which was given the name of his great victory and is still held from the Crown by the Dukes of Marlborough in petit sergeantry. This means that each year the duke has to give the Crown a token 'rent' which, in this case, is a little banner of the ducal coat of arms.

Vanburgh wanted to preserve the ruined palace as part of the landscape but Sarah, Duchess of Marlborough, disliked it and it was finally pulled down in 1723.

8

ROYAL TRANSPORT

Royal Yachts   *by Chris Ellis*

A familiar sight in newspaper pictures and TV newsreels on any state occasion or any overseas visit where Her Majesty Queen Elizabeth II travels by sea is that graceful and elegant vessel, gleaming in 'bluebottle blue' and white enamel, the royal yacht, H.M.S. *Britannia*. For all but the first two years of Her Majesty's reign, this handsome ship has steamed thousands of miles a year, mostly on official state business—fleet reviews, foreign state visits and so on—but sometimes on less arduous 'holiday' cruises, all in the service of Her Majesty or other members of the royal family.

The provision and manning of special ships, or 'yachts' for the personal use of the sovereign has been a Royal Navy responsibility stretching back well over 300 years and the present yacht, *Britannia* is believed to be the seventy-fifth such ship in Royal Navy service. In former times a reigning sovereign often had more than one yacht available, and, indeed, this is still reflected in the title of the admiral commanding the Royal Yacht Service who is known as Flag Officer Royal *Yachts*. In the last hundred years or so, royal yachts have had suitably regal names, but there are records of more light-hearted naming in the past. One of Queen Victoria's yachts was named *Fairy* in 1845, while Charles II had one of his yachts called *Fubbs*, which was the pet name of one of his mistresses. The same monarch, at the time of his restoration, purchased the coaling brig *Surprise*, an anonymous vessel which had carried him to exile in France, and this was refurbished and renamed, appropriately enough, *Happy Return*, to become one of the earliest royal yachts under the administration of the Admiralty. More suitably named was George IV's *Royal George*, a large and handsome vessel commissioned in 1817 which survived though not as a royal yacht—right up to 1905.

Best known name of all royal yachts is probably *Victoria and Albert*, the present *Britannia*'s immediate predecessor which was a classic example of its type from the 'golden age' of steam yachts—clean lines, clipper bow and stern, and tall masts and funnels. In fact, Queen Victoria reigned for so long that there were no less than three royal yachts carrying the name *Victoria and Albert* in her lifetime. The first of these became a secondary yacht, renamed *Osborne*, when a new '*V. & A.*' was commissioned in 1854. In 1870 another *Osborne* became the principal royal yacht, this vessel being a steam paddler. By the late 1890s *Osborne* had become quite outclassed by sleek new royal yachts built for the Kaiser and the Tsar of Russia. Victoria now felt that the old paddle yacht did not 'accord with her dignity as the head of a great maritime state', and allowance was made in the Navy Estimates for a fine new yacht which would match those of rival monarchs. The Queen suggested that the state apartments be made the same size as those in *Osborne* so that all the carpets and furniture could be re-used. In the meantime the Tsar had made available to the British Admiralty all the plans of his own new yacht *Standart* and the new ship—to be named *Victoria and Albert*—was a close copy of *Standart*. It was at this stage that fatal errors were made which led to the new '*V. & A.*' never being able to live up to her very elegant appearance. There was a mix-up in interpreting the displacement—metric and imperial measures were confused—and though the launch was successful in May 1899, completion of fitting out revealed that the vessel was disastrously unstable. To overcome the problem it was necessary to cut-down the funnels, remove the original forecastle (to reduce topweight), and add some 600 tons of concrete as extra ballast. All this nearly doubled the cost of the ship, up to the then very high cost of over £500,000.

Queen Victoria never used the new *Victoria and Albert*, and her successors to the throne made no more than minimal use of her. King Edward VII had a smaller more handy yacht built, H.M.S. *Alexandra* (named after his consort), commissioned in 1907 and used in preference to '*V. & A.*'. The latter ship was mainly restricted in use to very formal functions like fleet reviews, though she made one cruise to the Mediterranean in 1924 to take George V on holiday. By the time George VI ascended the throne in 1937 it was decided that a new modern vessel was required to replace the *Victoria and Albert*, and designs were prepared, with provision for the new yacht to be built under the 1939 Naval Estimates.

The second world war delayed the whole project at this point, and it was not until the post-war depression began to lift in 1951 that the idea was revived. At this time King George VI was in poor health and it was felt that a modern yacht able to cruise in warm climes would aid his recovery. Unfortunately this was not to be, and the King died the month that the order was placed with the builders, John Brown & Co. of Clydebank, in February 1952. The new yacht did continue one of the original 1939 ideas, that it should be dual purpose, used for royal functions in peace-time and suitable for rapid conversion to a hospital ship in time of war. The ship had to be able to operate in all climates, have a continuous sea speed of 21 knots (enabling her to operate with the fleet) and have a range of not less than 2,000 miles at 20 knots. The smallest economical vessel to meet these requirements was around 4,000 tons and just over 400 ft in overall length.

The keel of the new ship was laid in June 1952, she was launched, with the name *Britannia*, on 16 April 1953, and formally commissioned for service on 11 January 1954. Interestingly enough, the old *Victoria and Albert* stayed in commission right up until this time, before being scrapped, even though she had been laid up inactive at Portsmouth (used as an accommodation ship) since 1939. Some of the fittings and furnishings from '*V. & A.*' were used in *Britannia*, however, as an aid to economy.

Britannia is a very clean and graceful ship, looking like a miniature passenger liner. Much of the layout of the ship is obvious from external appearance, the entire after-section being available for the royal household. Between the main and mizzen masts on the shelter deck are the actual royal apartments, and these lead out on to a sun deck at the after-end of the shelter deck; this area is strengthened to act as a helicopter deck, less for royal use than for hospital ship use, since in modern warfare

[182]

most casualties would be transferred by air. At upper deck level, below the shelter deck, are state apartments (dining room, drawing room, ante-room and sitting rooms) with a main staircase down from the royal apartments above. Down a further deck, at main deck level, are cabins, sitting rooms and facilities for members of the royal household and guests. Below this, at lower deck level, are staff cabins, offices and facilities. A passenger lift serves the main, upper and shelter decks, in addition to stairways.

Engine room and accommodation for the officers and men occupy the forward end of the ship and follow usual Royal Navy practice. It is interesting to note that in the hospital ship role (fortunately not so far required), the accommodation for the royal party aft would become wards and operating theatres, for which they are ideally suited in size, and the royal galley and laundry would become the hospital galley and laundry; some 200 patients could be carried with a medical staff of about 60. Denny-Brown stabilisers are fitted to reduce rolling to a minimum in a seaway, and the ship is air-conditioned. The ships' boats are more numerous than in most naval vessels of this size, and include a 40 ft Royal Barge, two 35 ft medium-speed motor boats, a 32 ft motor cutter, two 27 ft motor whalers (as sea-boats), two motor dinghies and two sailing dinghies; at various times the personal sailing craft of H.R.H. Prince Philip have also been carried aboard. There is also a 'garage' to carry a royal Land Rover or limousine on overseas tours.

There are four accommodation ladders—starboard aft for the royal family, port aft for the royal household and callers, starboard forward for ship's officers and port forward for ship's company and stores. When royal personages are embarked there is a famous 'quiet routine'—no loudspeakers or shouted orders—and the men wear gym shoes. To ensure privacy no member of the ship's company works aft of the main mast after 0900 hrs. There are other unique customs; the ratings have a distinctive badge and cap ribbon, officers drink the loyal toast standing, not sitting as in other R.N. ships, and the royal yacht is the only R.N. ship commanded by an admiral, the Flag Officer Royal Yachts. The three masts (fore, main, mizzen) are necessary to allow for the tradition of dressing ship with flags or standards appropriate to the occasion. These vary greatly depending on the duty, personages embarked and whether

[183]

the ship is at a foreign or home port. Some typical combinations include the following:

H.M. The Queen embarked: foremast—flag of Lord High Admiral; mainmast—Royal Standard; mizzen—Union Flag (plus the Union Flag forward on the jackstaff and the white ensign aft on the ensign staff).

H.R.H. Prince Philip embarked only: foremast—Union Flag (the flag of an Admiral of the Fleet, Prince Philip's naval rank); mainmast—the Royal Standard; mizzen—the flag of another of Prince Philip's offices, typically but not necessarily the flag of the Elder Brother of Trinity House, (plus ensign and jack as before).

H.R.H. Princess Margaret embarked only: foremast—Vice-Admiral's flag (flag of Flag Officer Royal Yachts); mainmast—H.R.H.'s standard; mizzen—white ensign.

There are many other variations, including the practice of flying the flag or standard of a visiting head of state alongside the royal standard on the appropriate occasion.

In over twenty years' service H.M.S. *Britannia* has steamed thousands of miles the world over. She was not available for the greatest occasion of all, the Coronation Review at Spithead in 1953, being still under construction, and on that great day the Admiralty despatch vessel *Surprise* (a converted frigate) was adapted as a temporary royal yacht. Probably the longest single cruise was the world tour by H.R.H. Prince Philip, which included the famous Antarctica visit and in that year (1956) over 50,000 miles were steamed. When not engaged on royal duty, *Britannia* is usually based at Portsmouth, but she is sometimes involved in cruises which receive little publicity, such as proceeding to a foreign country ahead of Her Majesty so as to be on station (perhaps to provide accommodation) when the sovereign arrives from elsewhere, usually by air. On occasion, too, *Britannia* has exercised with the fleet, a typical role being to act as 'convoy' in an anti-submarine exercise.

Basic data: 3,990 tons standard, 4,715 tons full load, 360 ft (between perpendiculars), $412\frac{1}{4}$ ft (overall), 55 ft (beam), 16 ft (draught), engined by John Brown and Co with two shaft-geared turbines, 12,000 shaft horsepower giving 21 knots, two Admiralty-type 3-drum boilers, oil fuel—330–440 tons—two 3 pdr saluting guns. Complement—270 officers and men (reduced when royalty not embarked), and 52 (approx.) royal household staff (when royalty is embarked).

Royal Trains   *by O. S. Nock*

There was alarm throughout the land when it became known in the middle of June 1842 that the youthful Queen Victoria had made her first journey by train. The news came as a great surprise to nearly everyone. There was no preliminary announcement, in fact it was not until Saturday afternoon, 11 June, that Charles Saunders, the famous first Secretary of the Great Western Railway, was advised that the Queen, Prince Albert and their suite desired to travel from Slough to Paddington on the very next Monday—less than two days' notice! Fortunately the directors had anticipated that sooner or later the Queen would wish to travel by train, and two years earlier they had a royal saloon ready. Until 1842 it had been used by the Dowager Queen Adelaide. While the first journey of Queen Victoria was a great success, the public horror at such an 'adventure', by a mode of transport only thirteen years beyond Rainhill, was expressed in newspaper articles, the utterances of eminent statesmen, and in comments in parliament. The risks were considered too terrible to comprehend, and although an heir to the throne had been born the hazards of a long regency were stressed.

Providing the speed did not exceed 40 m.p.h. Queen Victoria enjoyed travelling by train, and from that first excursion used the railway frequently. Throughout her long reign however the times were very disturbed. The Chartist agitation and riots, the political unrest over the reform of the franchise, and above all Ireland, led to outbreaks of violence, and the running of Royal Trains was surrounded by measures of the closest security. An advance pilot engine was run fifteen to twenty minutes ahead of the Royal Train, and after its passage no shunting was allowed on adjacent lines; nothing else was allowed to pass on the route, and all points were clipped and locked. On the ordinary journeys of the Queen, between Windsor and London, between Windsor and Ballater (for Balmoral) and between Windsor and Gosport, when she was travelling to her Isle of Wight home at Osborne, the train was not decorated; but a magnificent show was put on by the Great Western Railway when Her Majesty travelled from Windsor to London in 1897, for the Diamond Jubilee celebrations. A new Royal Train had been built for the occasion, and it was drawn by one of William Dean's beautiful 7 ft 8 in 4–2–2 engines, specially named *The Queen*.

It was in the reign of King Edward VII that the London and North Western Railway built a truly sumptuous new train, specially for the annual royal visit to Balmoral. The King was asked if there was any particular styles in which he would like his own and Queen Alexandra's private saloons finished. He replied simply: 'Make it like a yacht.' King Edward had none of his mother's inhibitions about fast running, and when travelling to Edinburgh once by the East Coast route from Newcastle it was explained to him that one of the latest 'Atlantic' engines, one of the Smith four-cylinder compounds, would be hauling the train. His reaction was 'well show me what it can do'; and the driver did, arriving in Edinburgh ten minutes early, and before the official reception party had assembled to meet the King and Queen!

Upon the accession of King George V, in 1910, the L.N.W.R. named one of their latest engines *George the Fifth*, and happily it became the first of a famous and very successful class of 4–4–0s. In the following year one of them was named *Coronation*, and was used in connexion with special train workings to Caernarvon for the investiture of the Prince of Wales, in 1911. While trains conveying foreign royalty to London for the Coronation had decorated locomotives the British Royal Trains were not generally so adorned, except to putting a truly exhibition finish on the chosen locomotives. It was when King George V and Queen Mary visited India for the great Coronation Durbar at the end of 1911 that all the panoply and pageantry of the East was accompanied by some of the most magnificent decoration of locomotives ever accorded to the trains of a British monarch. The Great Indian Peninsula Railway, which had the honour of first conveying their Imperial Majesties after their arrival in India at Bombay, discarded their normal, very handsome engine livery of chocolate brown for a splendid royal blue, for every locomotive that would be concerned with the special workings—even the massive 0–8–4 tank engines that would bank the train up the formidable Ghat inclines.

[186]

Back in England, on the first occasion that a reigning monarch and his consort had visited a railway works—when King George V and Queen Mary so honoured Crewe in April 1913—the Royal Train from London was hauled by the engines *George the Fifth* and *Coronation*, and the advance pilot was the little 2–4–0 *The Queen*,★ which eighteen years earlier had made some very fast running in the Race to Aberdeen, in August 1895. But pageantry with British Royal Trains ended with the outbreak of war in 1914, except that from the 1920s the London and North Eastern Railway kept, at King's Lynn depot, two specially tuned and suitably embellished green 4–4–0s of the 'Super-Claud' class, for working the Royal Train when required between King's Cross and Wolferton, the nearest station for Sandringham.

On railways of the British Commonwealth there have been two very splendid Royal Trains both for King George VI and Queen Elizabeth. In 1939 there was a lengthy tour of Canada, and the Royal Train was run over many thousands of miles by both the Canadian Pacific and the Canadian National Railways. Both followed the Indian precedent of 1911, by giving the locomotives concerned special finishes in blue and silver. The occasion resulted in the rechristening, afterwards, of the 4–6–4, or 'Hudson' type used by the Canadian Pacific. For the tour the selected engine had royal crowns fixed on the running plate valences. After the tour His Majesty gave permission for the entire class to be named 'Royal Hudsons', and for the crowns to be affixed on all of them, which carried the standard C.P.R. livery of Tuscan red and black.

Finally, in readiness for the Royal Tour of South Africa in 1947, a most luxurious new train was built in England, and conveyed King George VI, Queen Elizabeth and their daughters on a 10,000-mile rail tour, beginning at Cape Town and extending as far north as the Victoria Falls and Salisbury, Rhodesia. It lasted just over two months, during which this beautiful 'White Train' was hauled by a great variety of British-built locomotives, with the heavy gradients often needing two Beyer-Garratts—always with a handsome rendering of the royal arms on the leading engine.

Today, when travelling on British Railways Her Majesty the Queen

★ Not to be confused with the Great Western 4–2–2 engine of the same name.

and her suite use the royal saloons built for her father and mother in 1941 for their special wartime journeys. These beautiful cars are marshalled with other vehicles as required, and hauled by diesel locomotives from the standard classes, as needed.

Royal Cars   *by G. N. Georgano*

King Edward VII was Britain's first motoring monarch, ordering his first car in 1900. His initial contact with road vehicles, however, took place forty years earlier, when he was only eighteen years old and asked to see one of the light steam carriages made by Thomas Rickett of Buckingham. It is not recorded that either he or his parents, Queen Victoria and Prince Albert, rode in the machine, but it was certainly the first time that a mechanically propelled road vehicle was demonstrated to British royalty. During the years of the Prince of Wales' young manhood and maturity there were no cars for him to enquire about, but when the new internal-combustion-engined machines began to come in from the continent in the 1890s he was not slow to show an interest. In February 1896 he rode in a German-made Daimler owned by the Hon. Evelyn Ellis, a pioneer motorist, and over the next three years he travelled in a number of cars owned by his hosts at various country houses. It was a drive with the Hon. John Scott-Montagu, son of the first Lord Montagu of Beaulieu that finally convinced the Prince of Wales, as he still then was, that it would be a good idea to own a car instead of merely riding in other peoples', and after further inspection of the Montagu car (a Daimler) in London, he ordered one himself, taking delivery in February 1900. The make was almost an inevitable choice for it was the best quality British car made at the time, and Edward had never ridden in any other make of car. It was unthinkable that he should commence motoring in a foreign car, although a few years later he became very fond of the Mercedes, and preferred the German make for unofficial journeys. The Daimler he chose was a two-cylinder 6 h.p. car equipped with a four-seater open body with canopy top. This was built by the old-established coach-building firm Hooper & Sons, who had been in business since 1805 and were to be responsible for the coachwork of most of the royal Daimlers until the 1950s.

By the time he came to the throne in January 1901 Edward had bought three further Daimlers, one a fourteen-seater 'beaters' car' used for grouse-shooting expeditions. The driver sat over the engine as in the Post Office vans which Daimler were building at this time, and the vehicle was more like a small bus than a private car. In May 1901 Queen Alexandra became a car owner in her own right when she ordered a light two-seater Columbia electric car. This had tiller steering and a maximum speed of 25 m.p.h. Alexandra used it mainly on the estate roads at Sandringham, and it is unlikely that she ever drove it on public roads. Edward himself did very little driving, although he soon became

King Edward VII's first motor drive on a public road, Warwick, 25 June 1898

[189]

a keen connoisseur of cars, and often asked his equerries to stop interesting cars on the road in order to discuss points of design with their owners. Both he and Alexandra were fond of speed, and the royal cars were apparently exempt from the prevailing 20 m.p.h. speed limit. In 1906 Edward was said to have exceeded 60 m.p.h. on the way to Brighton, although he was keenly aware of the dust problem, and gave orders that high speeds were not to be indulged in when the roads were dusty. Once when returning from Newmarket to London several of the King's friends followed the royal car closely, hoping that speed traps would be relaxed for the passage of His Majesty. 'But the constabulary were swift and ruthless,' said his mechanic Edward Stamper; all but two cars were stopped and their owners subsequently fined, including the Master of the Horse. Sir Henry Ewart, an equerry, suggested that the King must not be driven at more than 30 m.p.h., but Stamper thought that this would be difficult as His Majesty often gave orders for high speed, and he was afraid to disobey.

As the years passed, so the royal cars acquired the latest luxuries. A 35 h.p. Daimler landaulette of 1907 (the King's ninth Daimler) had a table, clock, barometer, speaking tube and electric light, as well as a speedometer in the passenger compartment. For his birthday Edward was presented with a silver-plated 'first aid' case containing scissors, bandages, lint, etc., and a sealed flask of brandy. All this was fitted into a small blue footstool which was transferred from car to car. Daimlers were still exclusively used for official occasions, although Edward favoured Mercedes for personal travel especially abroad, and Alexandra used Renault and Wolseley cars.

After Edward's death in 1910 the new king, George V, continued the Daimler tradition, using a 57 h.p. six-cylinder car that Edward had ordered but never rode in, and buying two more, one of which was fitted with a twelve-passenger shooting brake body. During his visits to the front in the first world war he normally travelled in army staff Vauxhalls, but after the war he ordered further Daimlers including some special models in 1923 which employed the enormous 57 h.p. engine of 1910, no longer available in regular Daimler cars. In 1928 George had a prolonged convalescence after a serious illness, and being particularly anxious to continue his favourite sport of shooting, he ordered from the Crossley company a special six-wheeled shooting car in which he could shoot while sitting down. The car was fitted with a lavishly equipped Hooper body, was capable of 60 m.p.h. over good roads and could travel comfortably over broken ground or ploughed fields.

Both George V and Queen Mary favoured cars with high roofs, and after her husband's death in 1936 Queen Mary continued to use a high Daimler limousine which was a familiar sight in London until she herself died seventeen years later.

After the second world war Daimlers continued to be the official royal cars; these were the DE36 straight-eight models which were fitted with closed or open bodies, the latter used on the royal tours of Australia and South Africa. However this model was no longer made after 1954, and as other Daimlers were much smaller machines unsuited to ceremonial occasions, the royal family had to turn to another make. Their choice was naturally Rolls-Royce, the leading British luxury car, and one which had been used by the Queen when she was Princess Elizabeth. The first royal Rolls-Royces were the very exclusive Phantom IV model, of which only eighteen were made, and all for heads of state, but when the Phantom V was launched in 1959 it was an ideal royal car. Nineteen feet ten inches long, with detachable moulded perspex roofs for use in parades, the Phantom V limousines with bodies by Park Ward are the 'flag ships' of the royal fleet of cars today. There are two of these at the Royal Mews, together with two older Rolls-Royces, and these four cars are the only ones in the country not required to display registration plates. The Queen always sits behind the chauffeur on the right, with a detective in the front passenger seat. When she is travelling in the cars her personal silver St George mascot is carried on the bonnet, but otherwise the cars wear the ordinary Rolls 'Flying Lady'.

Numerous other cars have been, and are, used by the royal family, in particular the Lagonda and Alvis convertibles favoured by Prince Philip in the 1950s and 1960s, a Rover 3·5-litre saloon which is the Queen's personal car, and Land- or Range-Rovers for country use. Both the Queen and Prince Philip are keen motorists and frequently drive themselves, a far cry from the days when George V wrote to his son (later Edward VIII and then Duke of Windsor): 'I must confess I do not approve of your driving a motor and have always said so ... it makes both Mama and me most anxious, as any little mistake and the accident occurs.'

It was only to be expected that Prince Charles and Princess Anne should be interested in cars, and both drove go-karts on private roads from an early age. Charles drove his mother a short distance at Windsor in a Vauxhall estate car when he was only thirteen years old, and passed his driving test at the age of eighteen and a half in a Rover 2000. His first car was an MG 'C' coupé, and he now owns an Aston Martin DB6. Princess Anne passed her test in April 1968, at the age of seventeen and three-quarters, and for her twentieth birthday received a Reliant Scimitar coupé from her parents and brother. She has since acquired another Scimitar, a GTE. The link between the royal family and this make was forged by Prince Philip when he used for a while a Scimitar with a special Triplex glass roof.

It will be evident that there has never been ostentation in the royal choice of cars, and indeed a feature from the earliest days has been to make cars last a long time, helped of course by meticulous maintenance. Pre-war royal cars lasted for an average of fourteen years, while the oldest Rolls-Royce in the fleet today dates back to 1950.

Four of the cars mentioned in this article can be seen by members of the public today: the 1900 6 h.p. Daimler and 1924 57 h.p. Daimler shooting brake (together with several other royal cars) in the car museum at Sandringham House, Norfolk, and the 1901 Columbia Electric and 1965 Reliant Scimitar Triplex coupé at the National Motor Museum, Beaulieu, Hants.

Royal Aircraft   *by Kenneth Munson*

Nowadays, it would be a matter for surprise if the royal family did not use air transport in the course of their official duties, but circumstances were very different half a century ago. Despite his disapproval (and, at times, his active discouragement), all four surviving sons of King George V, the 'Sailor King', became qualified pilots. Prince Albert (later Duke of York and King George VI) was the first, in 1919; but the prime mover in bringing the royal family into the air age was his elder brother Edward, then Prince of Wales.

Although he did not gain his licence until 1929, Prince Edward had by then been using R.A.F. or civil aircraft for some time to fly him, as a passenger, to various engagements. As a result, in May 1928 a Bristol Fighter (J8430) was officially assigned for his personal use, and was flown and maintained for him by No. 24 (Communications) Squadron at Northolt. The rear cockpit was upholstered for the royal passenger, and was fitted with dual controls and a large windscreen. The tail-fin bore a distinctive chevron marking, divided vertically and horizontally into alternate segments painted in the dark blue and red colours of the Brigade of Guards, and the wheel covers also were red. During the next few years the Bristol was followed by two Fairey IIIFs (K1115 and K1749) and a Westland Wapiti (J9095), all bearing generally similar markings.

For several years from the summer of 1929 there ensued a period of owning and flying light civil aircraft, joined (though to a lesser extent) by his brother George, later Duke of Kent. Between them the royal brothers owned at least half a dozen de Havilland Moths of various types, a Hawker Tomtit and a Comper Gipsy Swift. Then, in 1933, the Prince of Wales purchased the Vickers Viastra X, a twin-engined airliner. Registered G-ACCC (the 'double' last two letters having become by then a characteristic of the royal-registered aeroplanes), its fuselage sides sported panels in the now-customary 'Guards' red and blue, with silver trim lines. The wings and tail, and top and bottom of the fuselage, were also silver. There were veneered wall panels, safety glass windows and electrical heating in the soundproofed cabin, which contained six armchairs, tables, a cocktail cabinet, a gramophone and a typewriter. But, despite (or perhaps because of) its luxury, the Viastra was not greatly used by the Prince, who disposed of it in mid-1934 and replaced it by a four-passenger de Havilland Dragon (G-ACGG), which some claim was his favourite of all the royal aircraft. Be that as it may, it too was replaced in the following year, by a pair of Dragon Rapides (G-ACTT and G-ADDD).

Meanwhile, in July 1933 the base of the royal aircraft had been moved to Hendon, for easier access to and from central London. The wisdom of this move was emphasised when, after the death of King George V on 20 January 1936, both the Prince of Wales and the Duke of York were required to attend within 24 hours the Accession Council in London. The new King's personal pilot, Flight Lieutenant E. H. ('Mouse') Fielden, flew to Sandringham to collect them; and the Prince, as Edward VIII, thus became the first reigning British monarch to fly, his father never having done so. Shortly after his accession, in perhaps one of the most far-seeing acts of his short reign, Edward officially brought The King's Flight into being on 20 July 1936, with Fielden as its first Captain and the two Rapides as its first aircraft.

From then until the outbreak of war only one further aeroplane was added, but it was noteworthy in being the first royal monoplane with a retractable undercarriage: G-AEXX, an Airspeed Envoy III. This, too, was painted in a red, blue and silver livery, initially much the same as that of its predecessors, though a year or two after delivery the wings and tailplane were painted in red, with blue or black registration letters. With the outbreak of war, responsibility for operating the King's Flight Envoy reverted to No. 24 Squadron, though it did not serve much longer in its royal capacity. Three twin-engined de Havilland Flamingo transports (R2764, R2765 and R2766) were made available in 1940 to carry King George VI and Queen Elizabeth on official trips, but in 1941 The King's Flight was disbanded. Its aircraft helped to form a nucleus for No. 161 Squadron which, with No. 138 Squadron, was based at Tempsford from April 1942 under the command of Fielden, now a Group Captain. These two squadrons flew special-duty wartime missions, including the delivery of S.O.E. agents and supplies to various resistance movements, to no fewer than nineteen countries.

After the war, on 3 January 1947, The King's Flight was re-formed, with Fielden (by then an Air Commodore) once again its Captain. Now, however, it was newly located at R.A.F. Benson, near Oxford, and its aircraft were four brand-new Vickers Viking C. Mk 2s. Gone, however, were the colourful pre-war liveries: the royal Vikings were left in their natural (but *very* well polished!) metal finish, with standard R.A.F. insignia. Two (VL246 and VL247) were fitted out personally for the King and Queen, with dark blue carpets, pale beige upper cabin walls and ceilings, and dark beige leather-covered doors. There were two main lounge compartments, each with four adjustable armchairs (two facing forward and two aft) upholstered in pale blue; and each aircraft had a pantry, refrigerator and food heaters. The third and fourth Vikings (VL245 and VL248) served respectively as a 21-seat transport for the royal entourage and as a mobile workshop to maintain the other three. The Vikings' first major operation was the 1947 Royal Tour of South Africa, and one served at least until 1956, when it took the present Queen to West Africa. (The unit's title had, of course, become The Queen's Flight in 1952.)

The Vikings were succeeded by four four-engined de Havilland Herons, delivered in May 1955 (XH375), April 1958 (XM295 and XM296) and June 1961 (XR391). The first of these, a six-passenger C. Mk 3, with an extra navigator's position, became the Duke of Edinburgh's personal aircraft, and bore a band of Oxford blue on its fuselage. The other three Herons were eight-passenger C. Mk 4s, with green and grey furnishings. Herons XM295 and XM296 were delivered with an external scheme similar to XH375 but, following a much-publicised royal 'near miss', were later repainted in a bright 'missile red' scheme with a dark blue fuselage cheat line. The fourth Heron also bore this latter scheme when delivered. In later years, a green external trim was applied to the fuselage, engine nacelles and control surfaces of XH375.

It was the Duke of Edinburgh who, in 1953, first used a helicopter to fulfil engagements, and two Westland Whirlwind HCC. Mk 8 helicopters (XN126 and XN127) were added to the Flight in 1959. They were replaced by Whirlwind HCC. Mk 12s (XR486 and XR487) a few years later, and by the present (1976) five/ten-seat Wessex HCC. Mk 4s (XV732 and XV733) in 1969. Both the duke and his son, Prince Charles, are of course qualified pilots with licences which include a helicopter rating.

The present fixed-wing element of The Queen's Flight consists primarily of three Andover CC. Mk 2s, a V.I.P. version of the Hawker Siddeley 748 twin-turboprop airliner. The first two Andovers (XS789 and XS790) were delivered in mid-1964, and were joined by the third (XS793) some four years later. Their exterior livery is predominantly red and white, with a dark blue cheat line along the fuselage sides; internally, blue is the predominant colour, dark for the carpets and pale blue or a mixed pattern for upholstery and curtains. The Andovers have a four/six-seat royal lounge aft, a second eight/ten-seat lounge

[195]

Cabin of a Hawker Siddeley Andover of The Queen's Flight

amidships, and provision for a further four crew seats and luggage pannier in the forward compartment. This is the normal configuration, but the seating layout can be varied up to a maximum of thirty-two passenger seats.

Since its formation in 1936 The King's/Queen's Flight has had only four Captains. Fielden, as Air Vice-Marshal Sir Edward H. Fielden, G.C.V.O., C.B., D.F.C., A.F.C., served until 1962 when he was succeeded by Air Commodore A. D. Mitchell, C.V.O., D.F.C. and Bar, A.F.C., who in turn was followed by Air Commodore J. H. L. Blount, D.F.C. Since Blount was killed, in the crash of one of the Flight's Whirlwind 12s which suffered a mechanical failure on 13 December 1967, the Flight has continued under its present Captain, Air Commodore A. L. Winskill, C.V.O., C.B.E., D.F.C. and Bar.

9

THE ROYAL FAMILY TODAY

On the occasion of their silver wedding, the Queen and the Duke of Edinburgh gave a party at Buckingham Palace for some of the members of the royal household, representing every department in it. Dukes and footmen joined together to congratulate the royal couple, wish them *ad multos annos* and make a presentation on behalf of the whole household.

I mention this because, for the first time, I realised just how large and diverse a body the household really is proudly serving, in a myriad ways, the family which personifies and unites the nation.

I am one who has little time for those who make outspoken and usually ill-informed criticisms of our monarchy. In the past there have frequently been occasions when the behaviour of the sovereign rightly attracted criticism, even odium, but for the last hundred years our royal family has fulfilled its role, which is always subtly changing, in a way that has earned our country the respect and envious glances of the modern world. If the media do not always put across an acceptable image of monarchy (to use the jargon of the day) it is hardly the Queen's fault. The Press Office at Buckingham Palace do their best to inform and assist journalists, but in the final analysis what is published reflects the views and prejudices of the writers and broadcasters. It is true that the Queen herself cannot answer attacks on the monarchy, but this is no real hardship as she has able protagonists who, like knights of old, will defend her against her enemies both at home and abroad.

Just consider for a moment the weight of responsibility which rests upon the Queen's shoulders. Not only is she the sovereign and visible head of the British Commonwealth, but also the head of the armed forces and the Supreme Governor of the Church of England. She has only to make a small error of judgement, or say an incautious word and irreparable damage could be done to the monarchy and the country. There is much truth in those oft-quoted lines from the dedication of Lord Tennyson's *Idyll of the King*:

> '*Wearing the white flower of a blameless life,*
> *Before a thousand peering littlenesses,*
> *In that fierce light that beats upon a throne.*'

For not only is the Queen expected never to stray from the straight and narrow path, but she and her family are also expected to be models of correct behaviour, family unity and exemplary morality, not just according to the canons of the Church of England, but according to such rules and moral strictures as other religious bodies or groups may consider important. For example, when the Queen attended a race meeting on a Sunday there were howls of protest from a small minority who considered this morally reprehensible.

Nor is this onerous weight of responsibility the only burden the sovereign must bear. Irrespective of her personal feelings and interests, she is expected to fulfil a vast number of engagements, constantly meeting people and having to put them at their ease. Consider the royal Garden Parties alone. On these occasions, the Queen has to appear before about eight thousand people, many struggling to get near enough to her to take home a memory of the day they saw the Queen. Her every move and gesture, and every word she utters are noted by thousands of curious eyes and ears. Even when she eventually gets her cup of tea, hundreds of her guests crowd round the enclosure and gape at her. It is scarcely a relaxed tea party.

Think too of her mornings, when she has to work through stacks of official papers which are showered upon her by the Cabinet and Government Offices and then having to receive innumerable dignitaries in audience, frequently being constrained to conduct tedious conversations through interpreters. It might be fun to do once, twice or even a hundred times, but day after day, inexorably, relentlessly and all excuses set aside; it is a formidable prospect. She is never able to escape from those red despatch boxes which seek her out wherever she may be.

In the same way, it might be exciting to be the Queen for a year, going on state visits and entertaining heads of state in this country, even if your hosts and guests were more or less unknown quantities, possibly not even speaking the same language; but the excitement must begin to pall after the first few years. The Queen and the Duke of Edinburgh have made state visits to Norway, Sweden, Portugal, France, Denmark, Holland, Nepal, Japan, Iran, Turkey, the United States of America, Italy, the Vatican, Ethiopia, the Sudan and the Federal German Republic, to name only some of the countries visited. They have toured the Commonwealth, frequently visiting the major Commonwealth countries, where they have attended festivals, the Queen has opened parliaments and she and her consort have worked relentlessly to help to bind together that family of nations called the Commonwealth. In this task they have not always been assisted by the politicians, some of whom seem to take a very cavalier view of the unity of the Commonwealth. But, if an united Commonwealth is considered to be a good thing, then the existence of a supra-political, unelected head is, to my mind, essential. If that head is also prepared, as the Queen is, to devote herself selflessly to the good of that Commonwealth, by constantly involving herself and her family in its daily life, then this is a bonus for which those of us who believe in a strong Commonwealth must be humbly and sincerely grateful.

I have mentioned the Queen's family deliberately because it must never be forgotten that they all help to bear the burden of sovereignty. They, too, are forever making public appearances, opening events, visiting and helping to raise money for charity. Obviously, some of these occasions must be most enjoyable, although constantly being on one's best behaviour must necessarily take the gilt off any gingerbread, but at other times it must be deadly boring. I once saw a member of the royal family at an event where she was feeling distinctly unwell, depressed and bored. Yet I did not observe this, I only knew it because I learned about it afterwards. At the time she was smiling and talking and evincing an interest in a way which could have won her a lead part on the London stage. The royal family has an enormous sense of duty and occasion which, combined with a remarkable team spirit makes the present 'royals' genuinely beloved of the population. It would be of more than academic interest to know how much, in hard cash, is raised for charity each year by the patronage and presence of members of the royal family. I suspect that every penny paid towards the upkeep of our monarchy is returned with interest to the poor, the old and the needy. It is a sobering thought and one which critics of the cost of maintaining the monarchy would do well to ponder.

All these manifold activities of the royal family are ably organised by the household. There is the formal household which, as it were, provides a suitable backcloth for royalty. It does not do much but, almost on the basis of Parkinson's law, it adds to the dignity of the crown and dignity is as important as affability. No one respects a person who lacks human dignity and in the same way, the crown would lose a vital element if it were stripped of all the trappings of royalty. So there is a battery of Chaplains to the Queen, Chaplains in Ordinary and Extra Chaplains, Extra Gentlemen Ushers, Physicians, Extra Physicians and Extra Equerries, but there are also some key men in the household whose duties are far from nominal.

To many, the Lord Chamberlain is simply a censor of plays. In fact, this unpopular task, like various other less controversial duties, are no longer his care. At one time his office was concerned with débutante presentations at Court, levées and drawing rooms, but these tedious, formal functions are now no more. Today the Lord Chamberlain is responsible for much royal ceremonial, Garden Parties, and a host of other lesser matters.

The Master of the Household looks after the day to day domestic running of the household whilst all transport arrangements are in the hands of the Crown Equerry, who technically comes under the Master of the Horse, the Duke of Beaufort. The Treasurer, Comptroller and Vice-Chamberlain of the Household and also the Captains of the Honourable Corps of Gentlemen at Arms and of the Queen's Bodyguard of The Yeomen of the Guard are all political appointments, the actual work being done by permanent officials. Of these quite the most important and influential is the Queen's private secretary. Her finances are in the care of the Keeper of the Privy Purse and the officials in his office, rather than the politician who holds the appointment of Treasurer.

Although the Court still counts among its members holders of offices with splendid names and long histories, such as the Hereditary Grand Almoner, the Poet Laureate and the Hereditary Keeper of Holyrood, there are other less glamorous offices which show that the Court, though still haunted by the ghosts of former glories, is essentially an up to date and highly efficient organisation.

Today the royal family jets and chops all over the world. One of the most important offices in the Palace is not some romantic-sounding body like the Board of the Green Cloth, but that of the Press Secretary, who treads a delicate path between guarding the Queen's privacy and keeping the media fully informed on matters of public interest. The Lord Steward of the Household no longer has other than ceremonial duties to perform, being superseded, at least in some practical aspects, by the shop steward of the palace branch of the Civil Service Union!

It would be pointless having an efficient, modern household if the royal family did not themselves adopt an up-to-date attitude towards life. This they have certainly done, yet without losing that mystique and dignity which, consciously or subconsciously, the Queen's subjects expect. The Queen's informal lunch parties have been a great success and the film recently made on the royal family has brought it home to people that in spite of all the ceremonial and protocol, they are also able to live ordinary, normal, albeit fairly hectic lives. The patronage of youth and conservation by the Duke of Edinburgh and his easy 'off the cuff' manner, which the Prince of Wales has happily inherited, give the family a whole new dimension.

Critics of royalty like to suggest that princes and princesses are usually blest with limited intelligence due to excessive inbreeding and that if they have thoughts these do not bear examination. That is, in any case, an absurd view and one which is utterly confounded by the clear and logical minds, intelligence, wide knowledge, wit and ability of the Queen, her husband and her family.

If it is obvious how hard the royal family work, how do they relax? The traditional sport of kings was the chase. Hunting the stag, or the boar was what all kings were expected to do and certainly did. Jousts and tilts were also popular as was hawking, particularly with the women. Henry VIII introduced tennis and tennis courts became a feature of his palaces. King Edward VII disbanded the royal buck hounds, but this was perhaps not too great a sacrifice as his favourite sport was shooting, as was that of his son King George V, who was a splendid shot and was also a keen big game hunter when the opportunity presented itself.

King George VI shared his father's love of shooting and also, to a great extent his ability, although I do not believe he ever equalled George V's record of bringing down four birds with a single shot. He also enjoyed riding to hounds and was an able tennis player.

Recent monarchs have been interested in horse racing but none has had quite the love of the turf evinced by the Queen and her mother. By happy chance, their patronage is nicely divided, as the Queen favours flat racing whilst the Queen Mother races under National Hunt rules. In February 1976 her many admirers shared her joy at leading in her three hundredth winner.

The Queen enjoys anything to do with horses and so is able to share in the excitement of the eventing and show-jumping successes which Princess Anne and her husband have had. She also takes pleasure in watching polo, a favourite sport of Prince Charles and, until recently, of his father as well, who has now given it up in favour of the less physically demanding but equally exciting sport of driving.

Naturally, the likes and dislikes, comings and goings, abilities and interests of the Prince of Wales must always be the subject of popular concern and curiosity. For it is he who, in the normal course of events, will eventually be called upon to undertake the full and onerous duties of sovereignty. If inherited characteristics count for anything, he is singularly well endowed; if careful training, together with a broad and catholic education help to determine a man's outlook and balance his character, he lacks for nothing and if the promise of the last eight years of public life are fulfilled, we should one day have a king able and worthy to succeed an exceptional Queen and, like her, to command the affection, admiration and loyalty of hundreds of millions of people.